Artist Eugene J. Martin's 2000 Acrylic Paintings on Canvas

Suzanne Fredericq

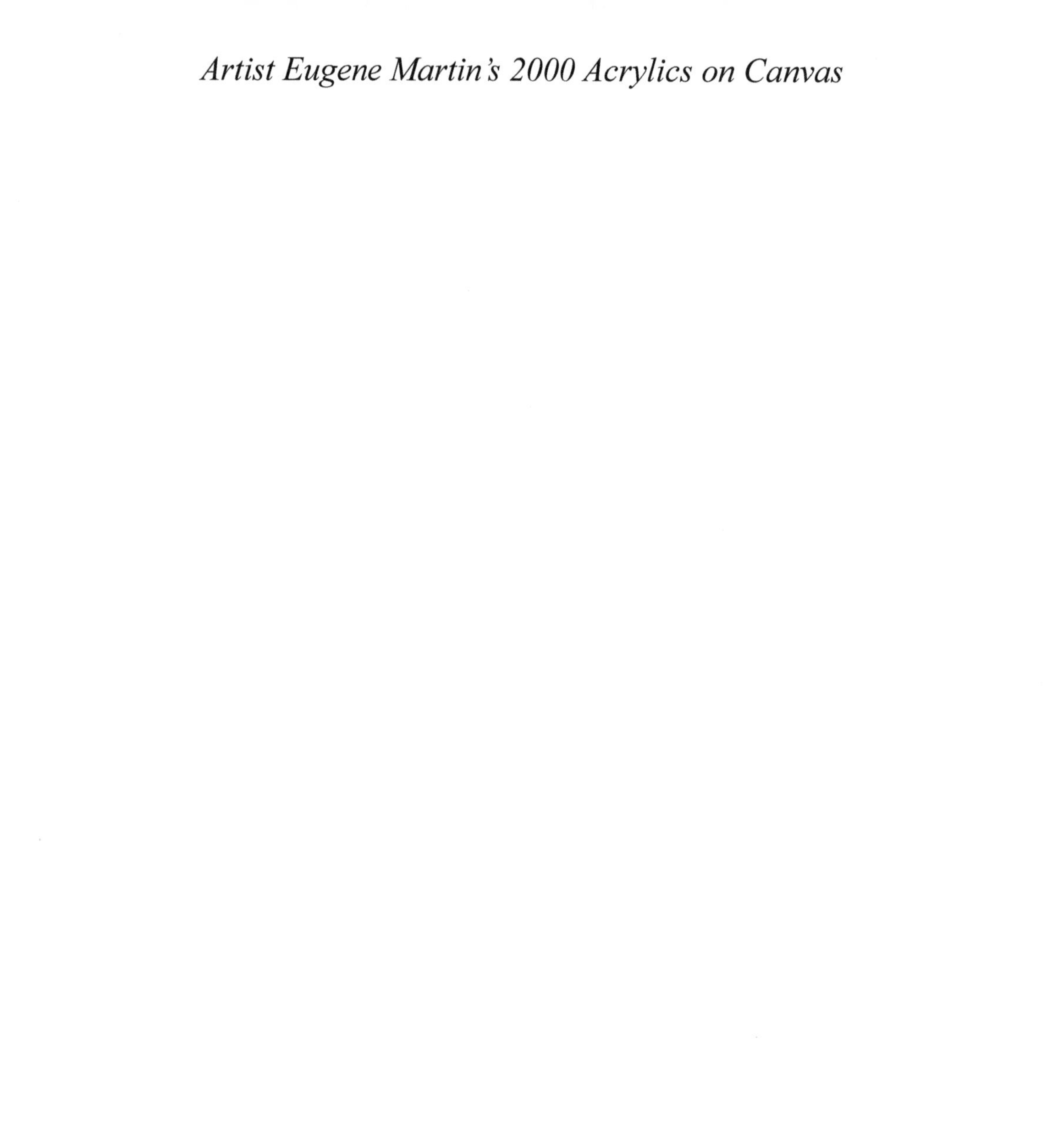

ISBN: 978-0-9825704-7-0

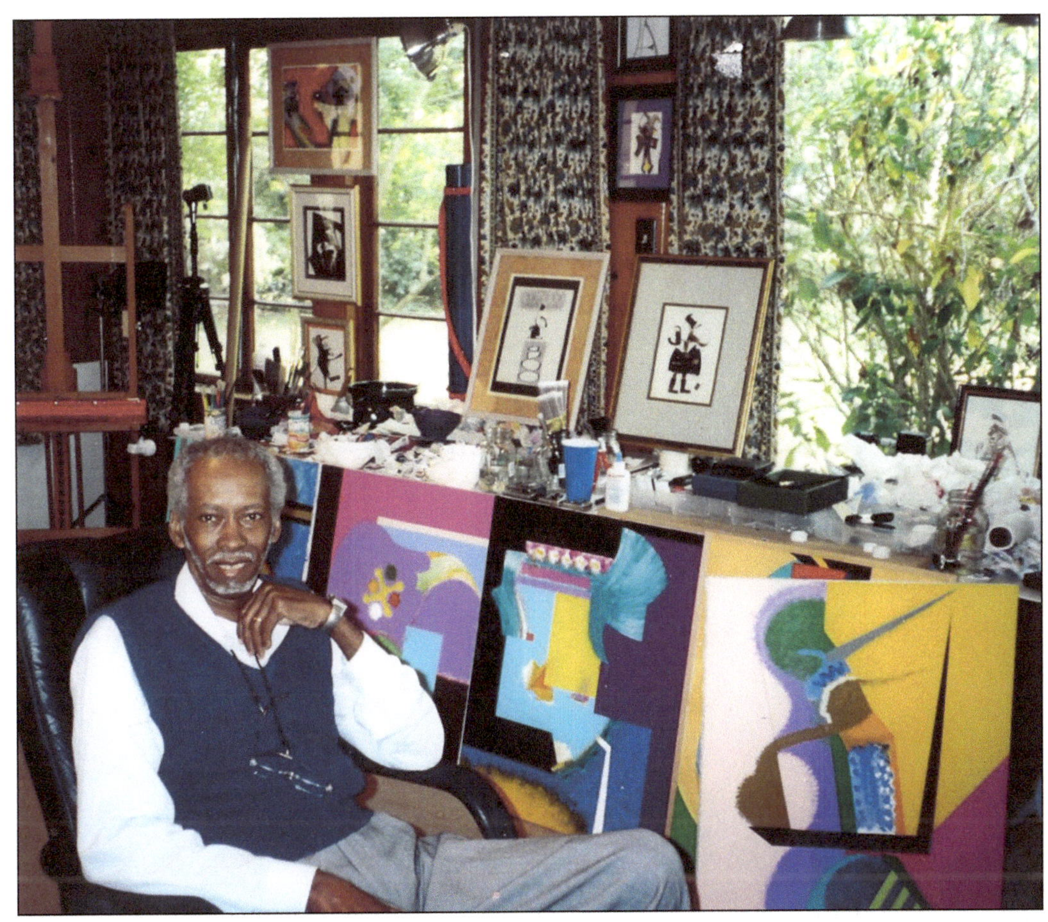

Eugene Martin in 2000, sitting in his studio in Lafayette, Louisiana, with three unfinished acrylic paintings on canvas showcased in this publication

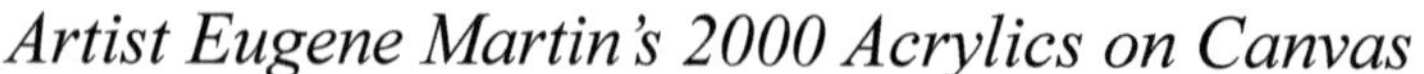

Foreword

This compilation includes reproductions of thirty-two abstract acrylic paintings on canvas painted by artist Eugene James Martin in his studio in Lafayette, Louisiana, in 2000. All works measure 24x30" (~76 x 60 cm)

Suzanne Fredericq,

Lafayette, Louisiana, November 26, 2009

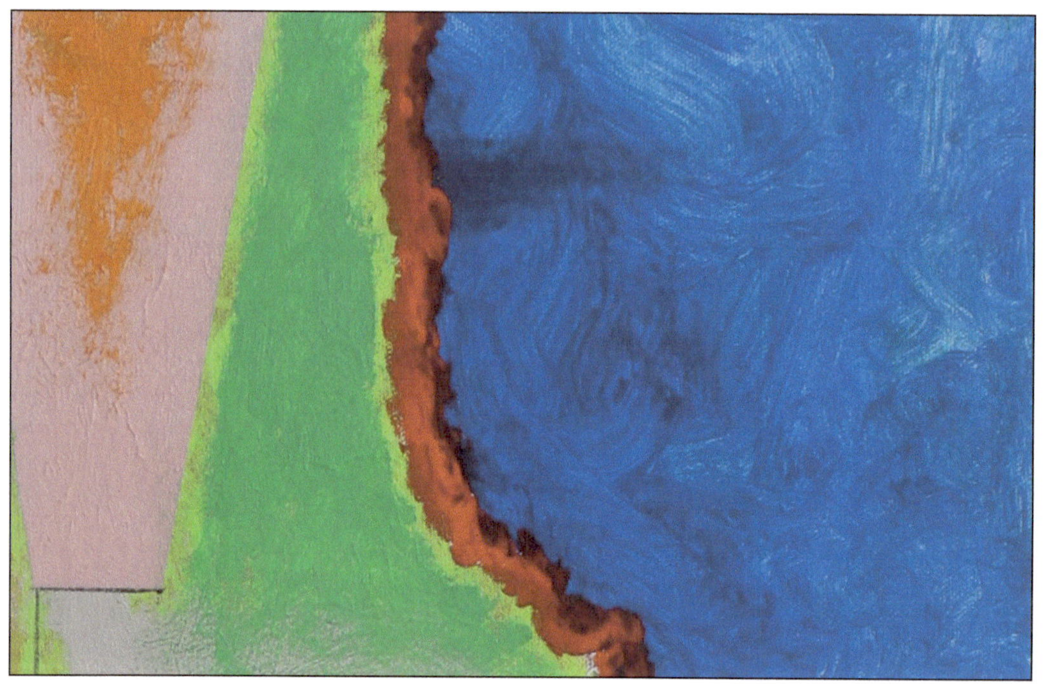

Untitled, 2000, acrylic on canvas (at right, close-up above), 30x24"

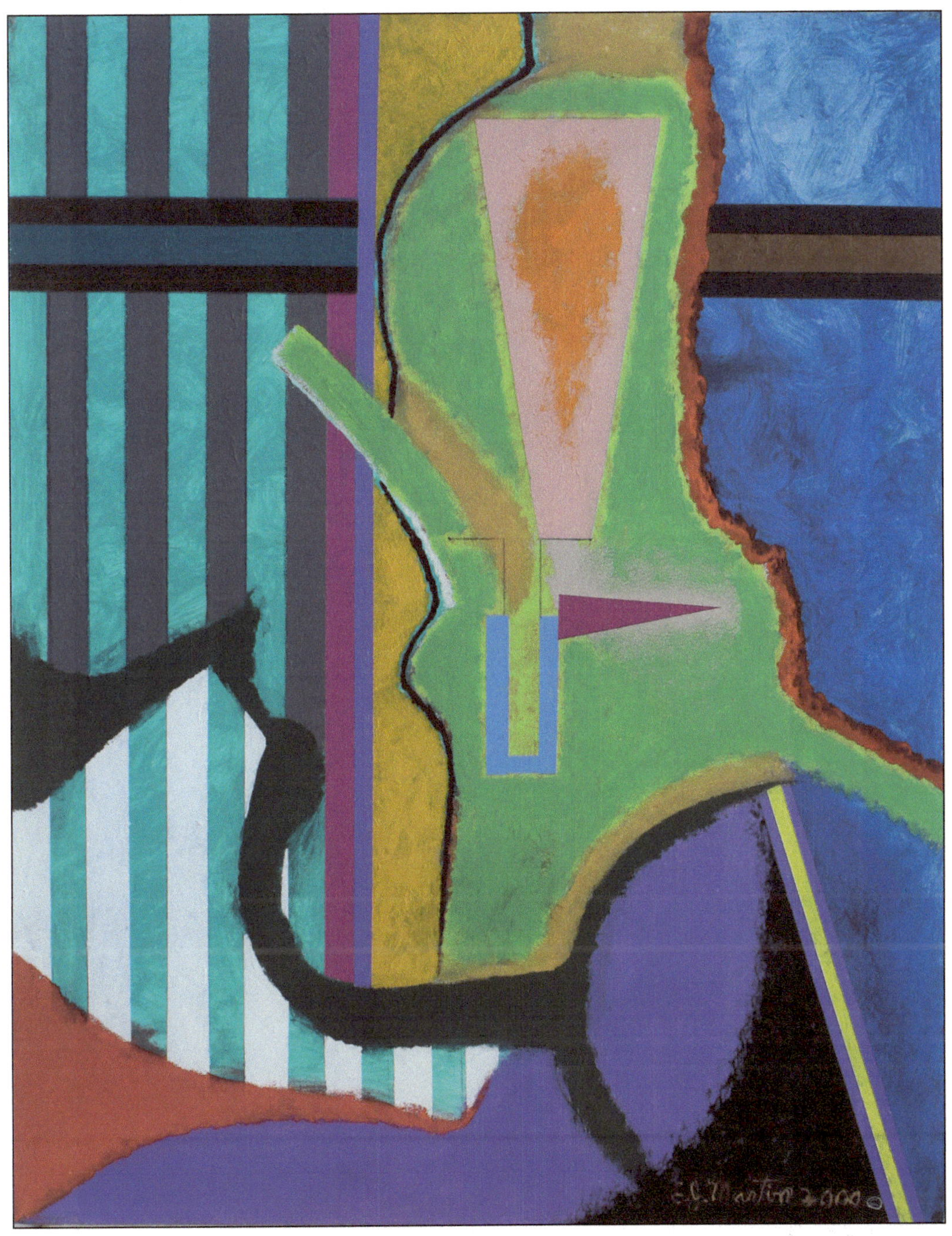

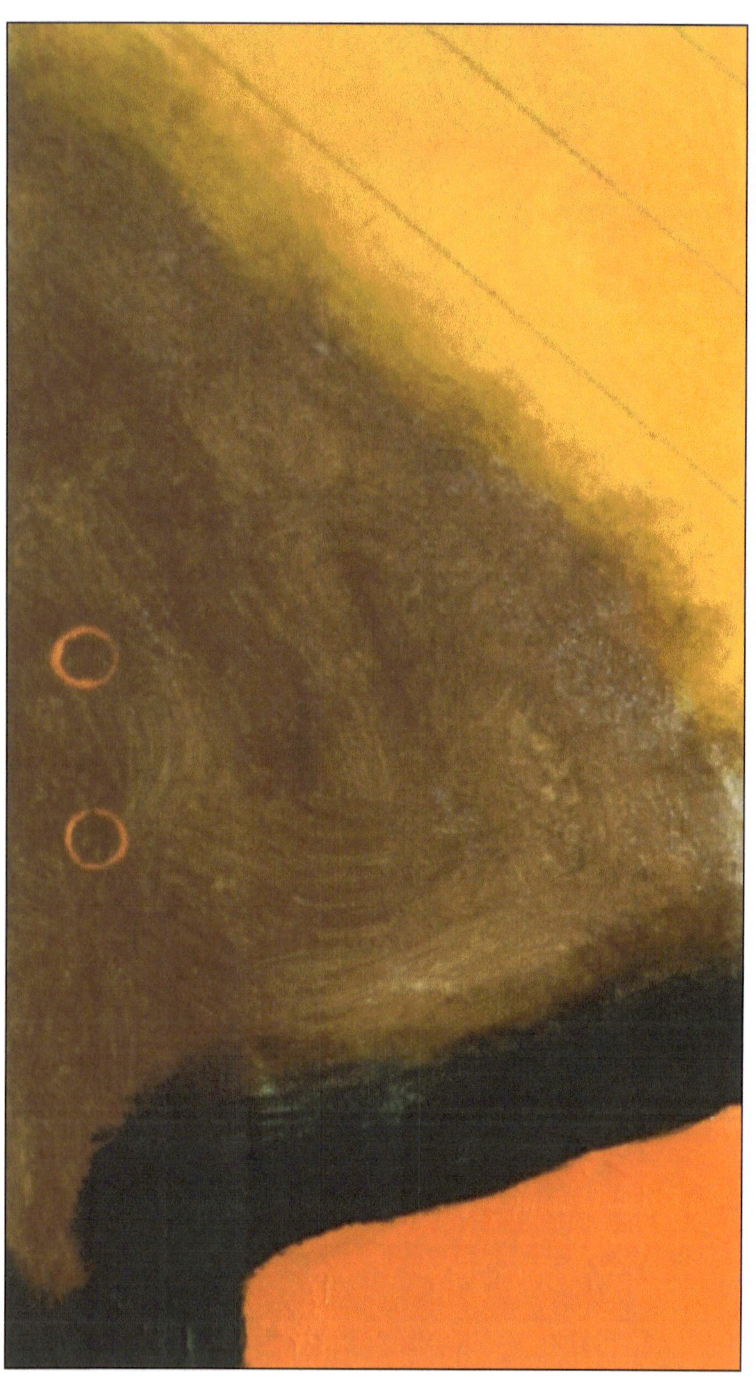

Untitled, 2000, acrylic on canvas (at right, close-up above), 30x24"

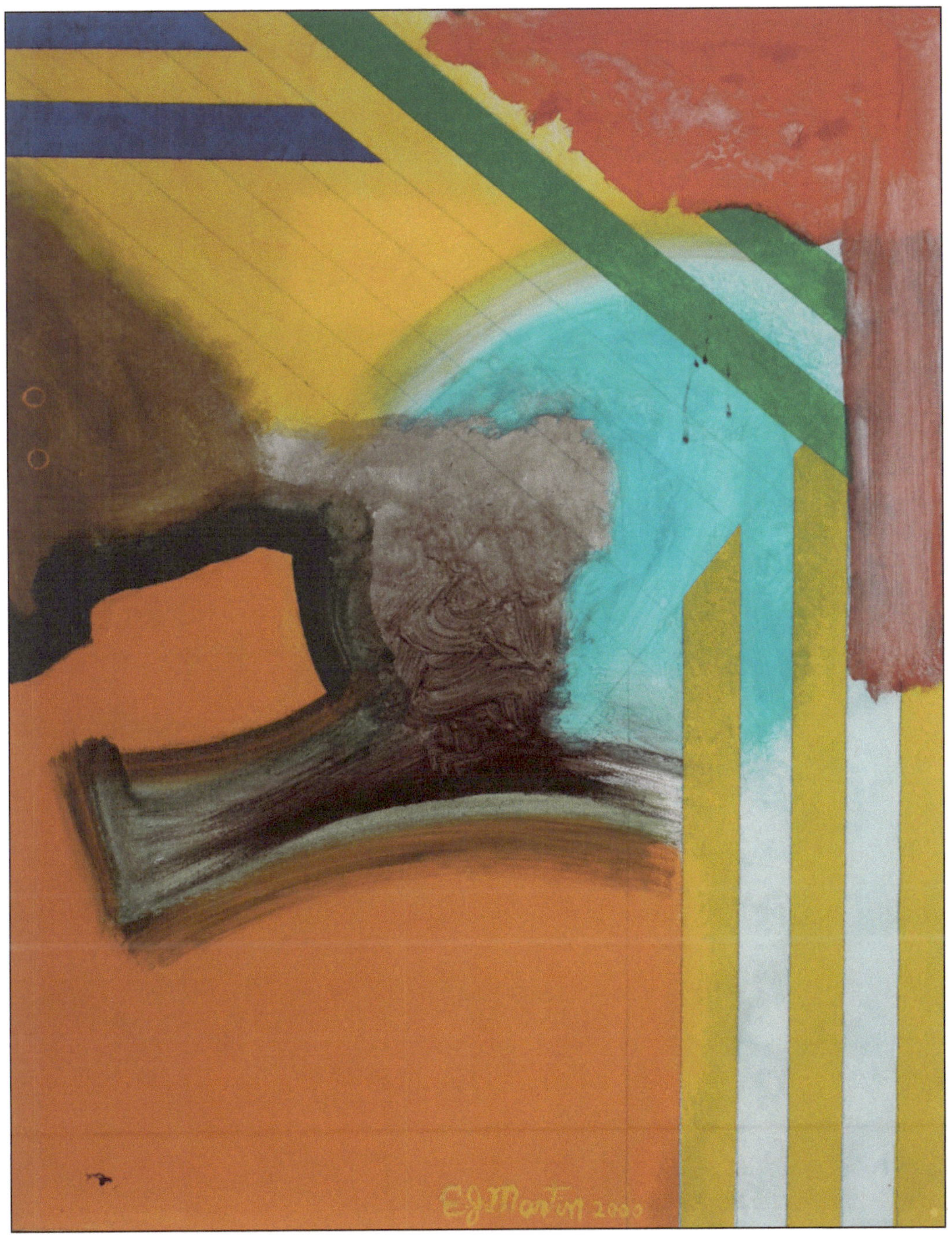
EJMartin 2000

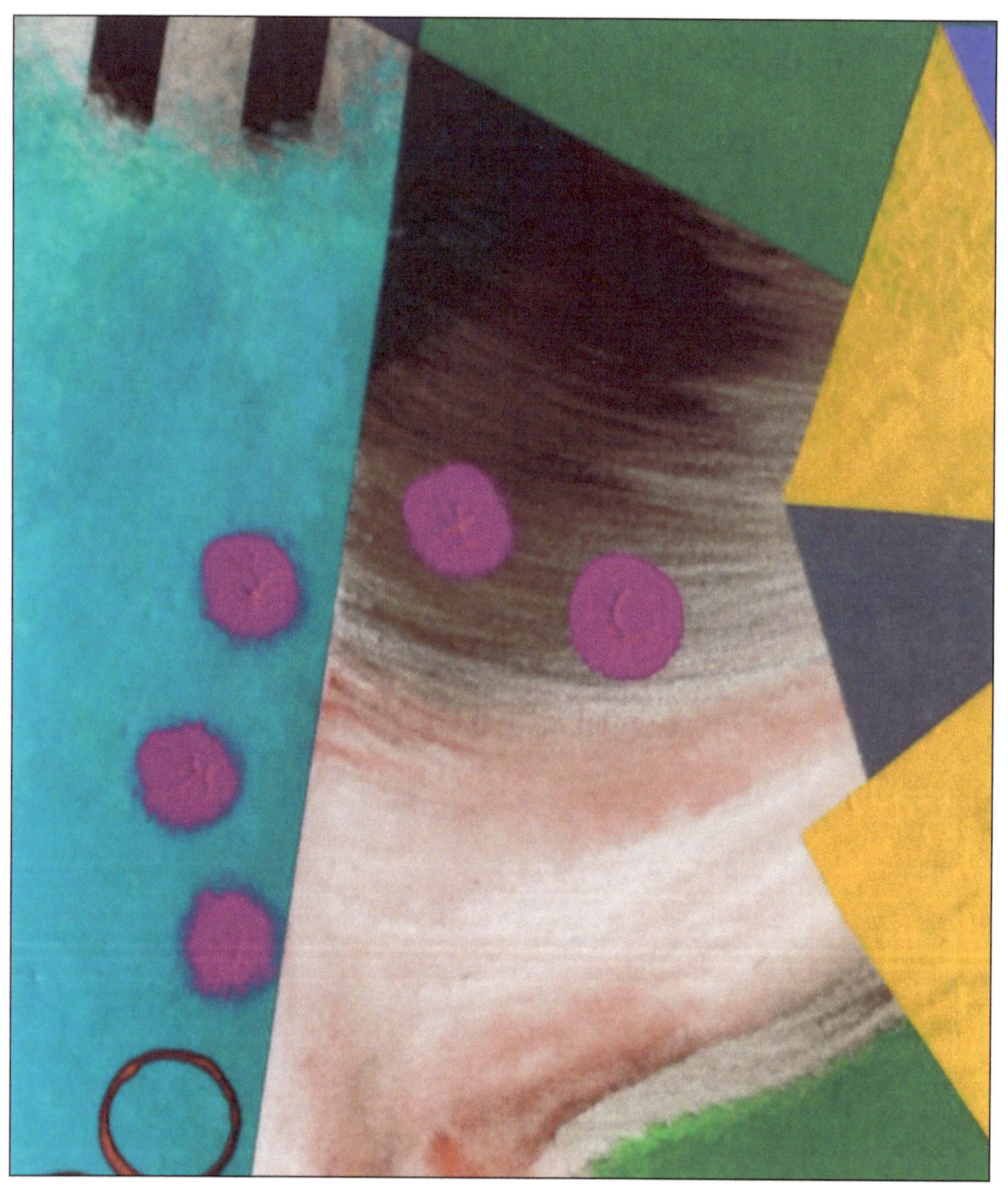

Untitled, 2000, acrylic on canvas (at right, close-up above), 30x24"

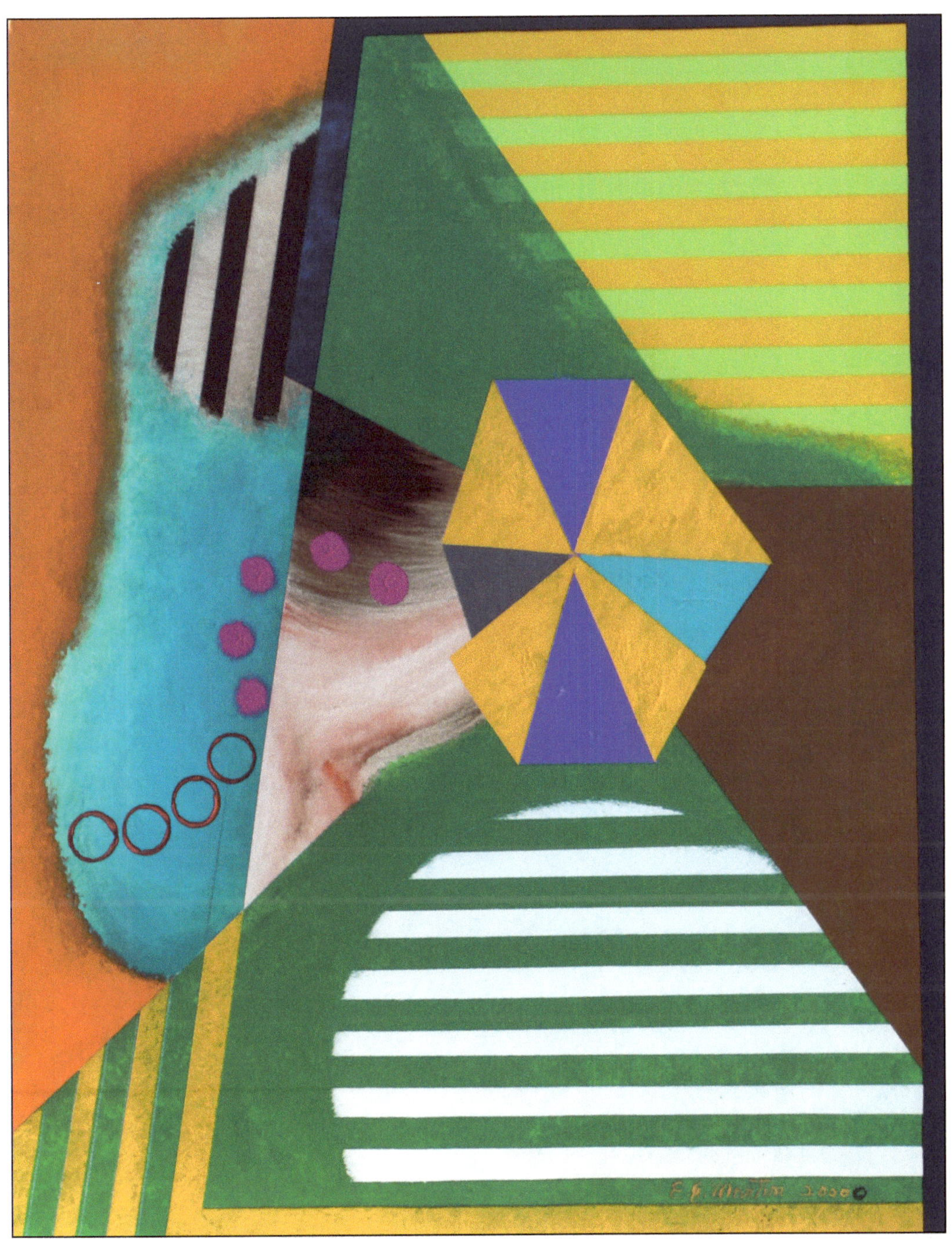

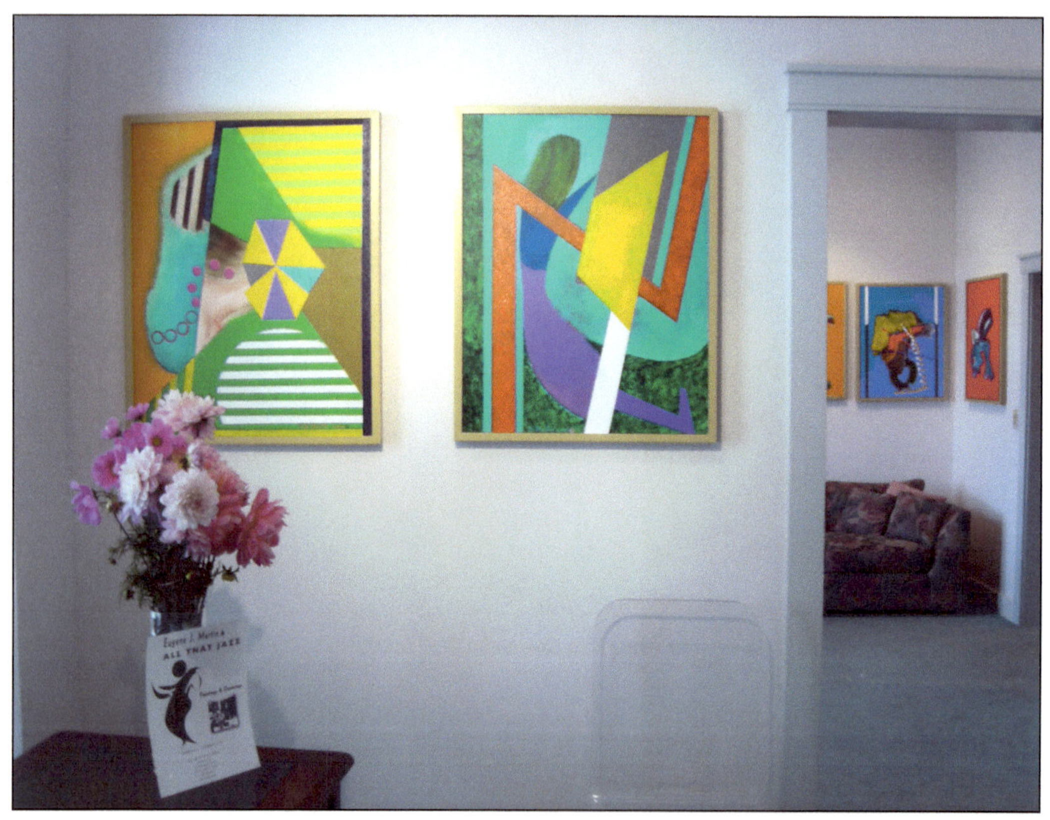

Untitled 2000 acrylic painting, showcased on p. 11, exhibited at the 2006 Eugene J. Martin: All That Jazz Exhibit at the Stowitts Museum in Pacific Grove, California

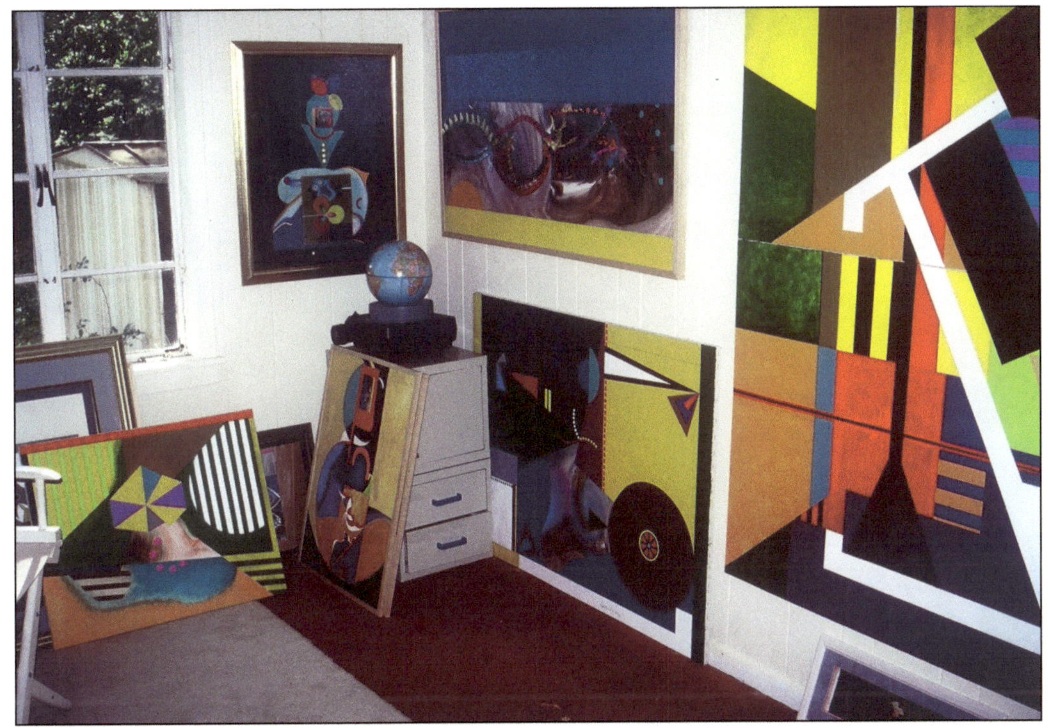

Untitled acrylic painting, showcased on p. 11, among other artworks in Eugene Martin's studio in Lafayette, Louisiana

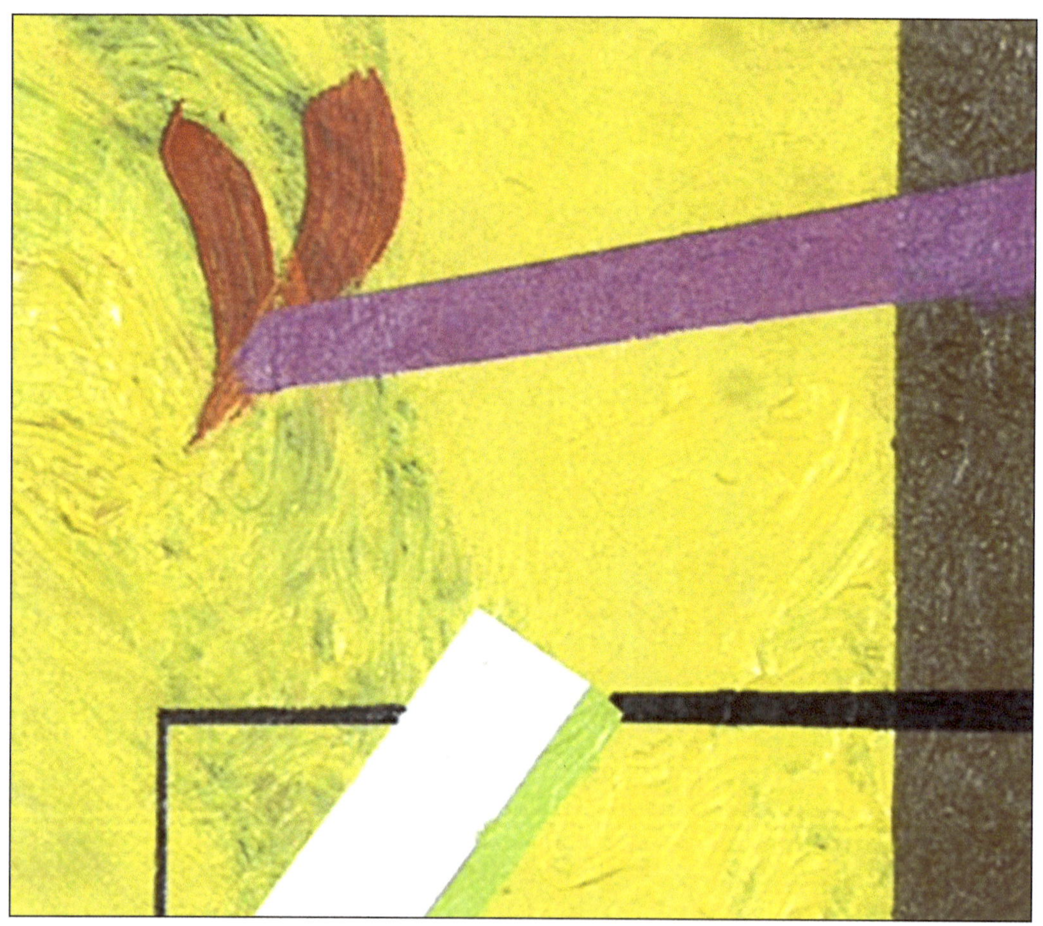

Untitled, 2000, acrylic on canvas (at right, close-up above), 30x24"

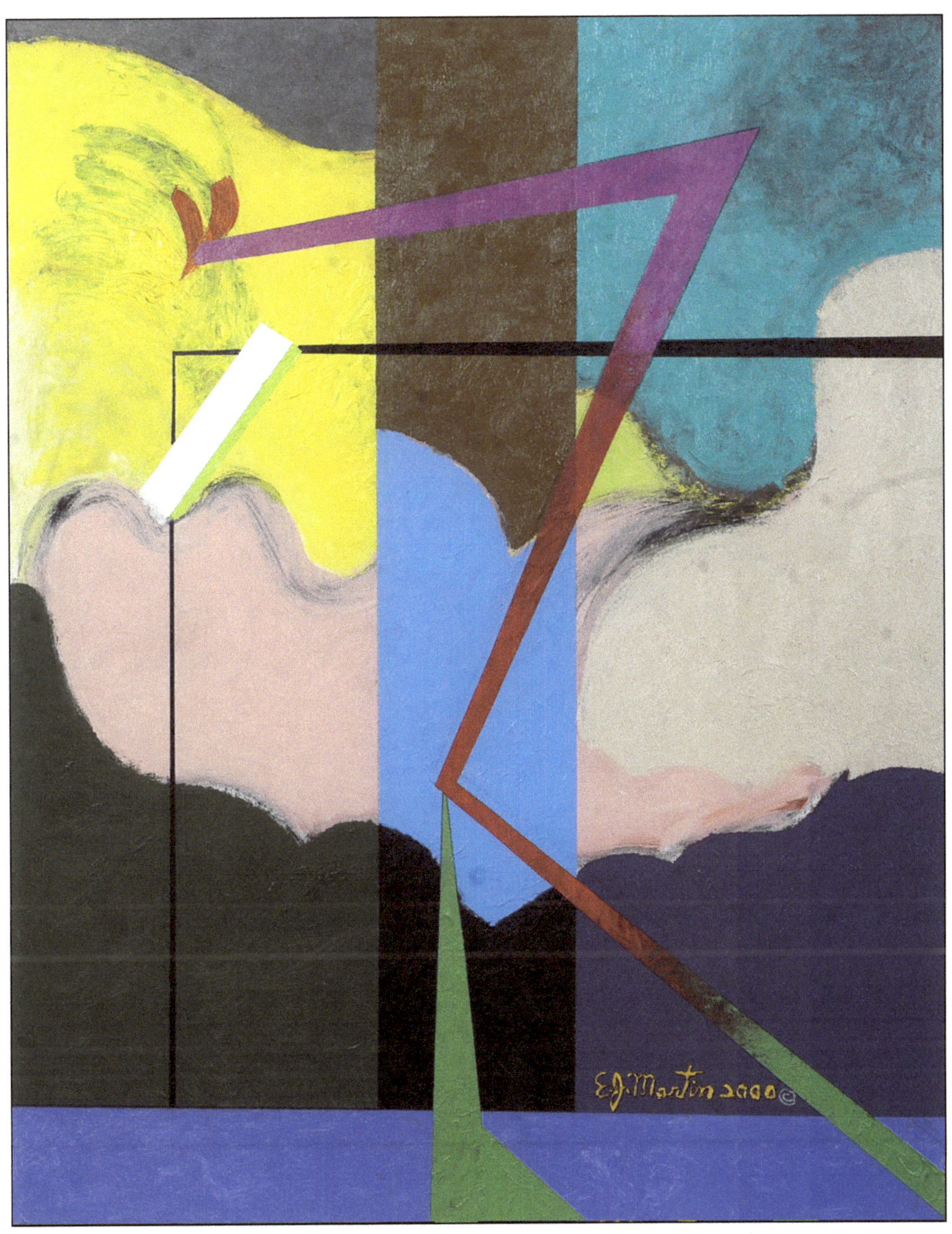
E.J. Martin 2000©

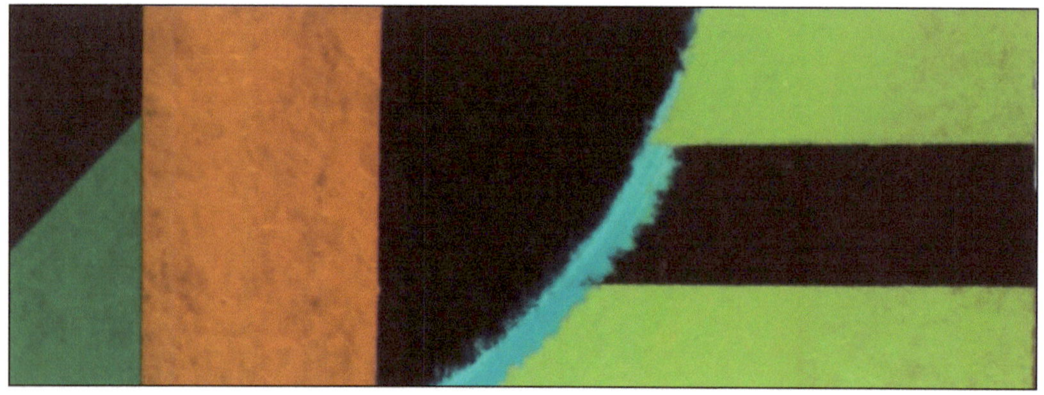

Untitled, 2000, acrylic on canvas (at right, close-up above), 30x24"

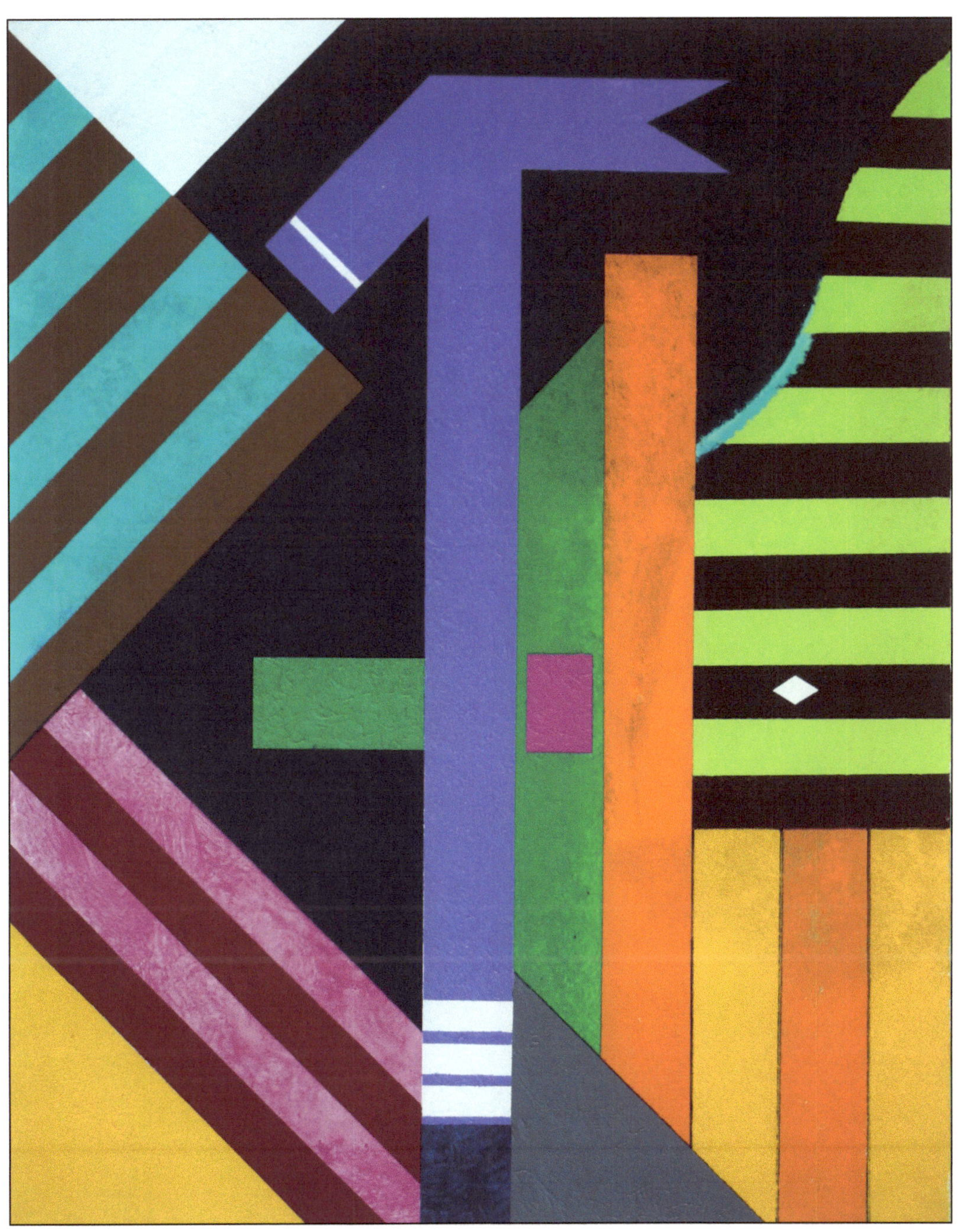

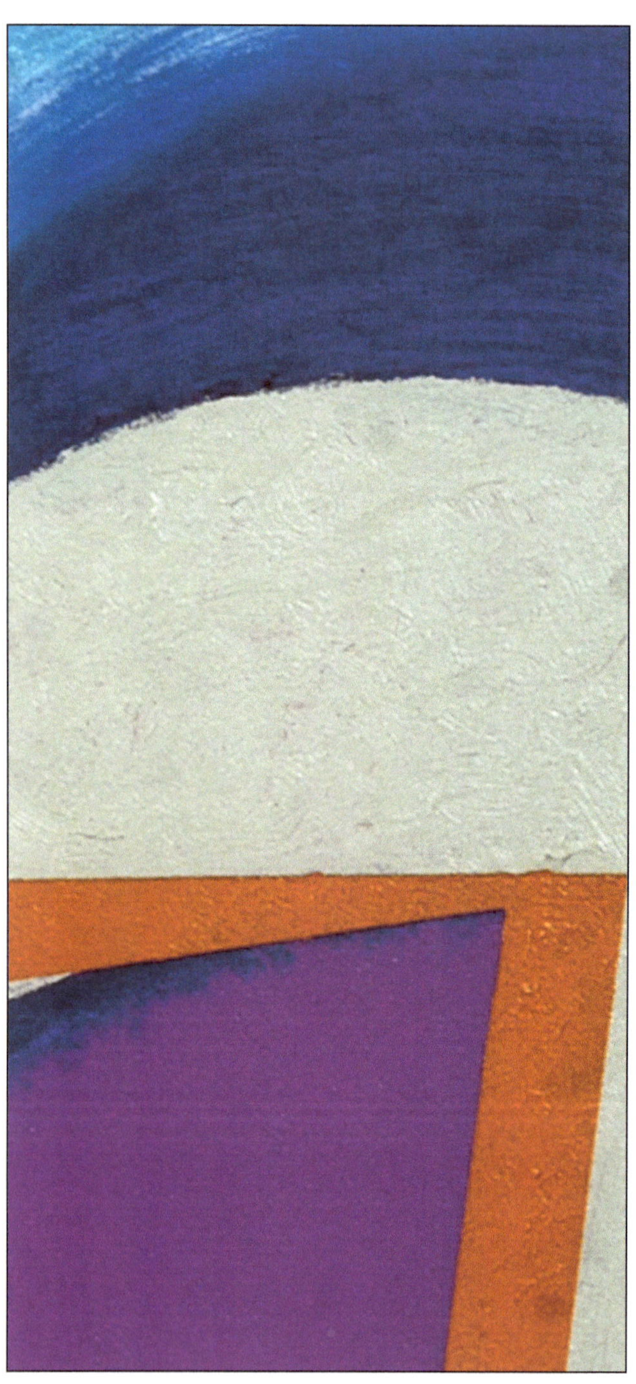

Untitled, 2000, acrylic on canvas (at right, close-up above), 30x24"

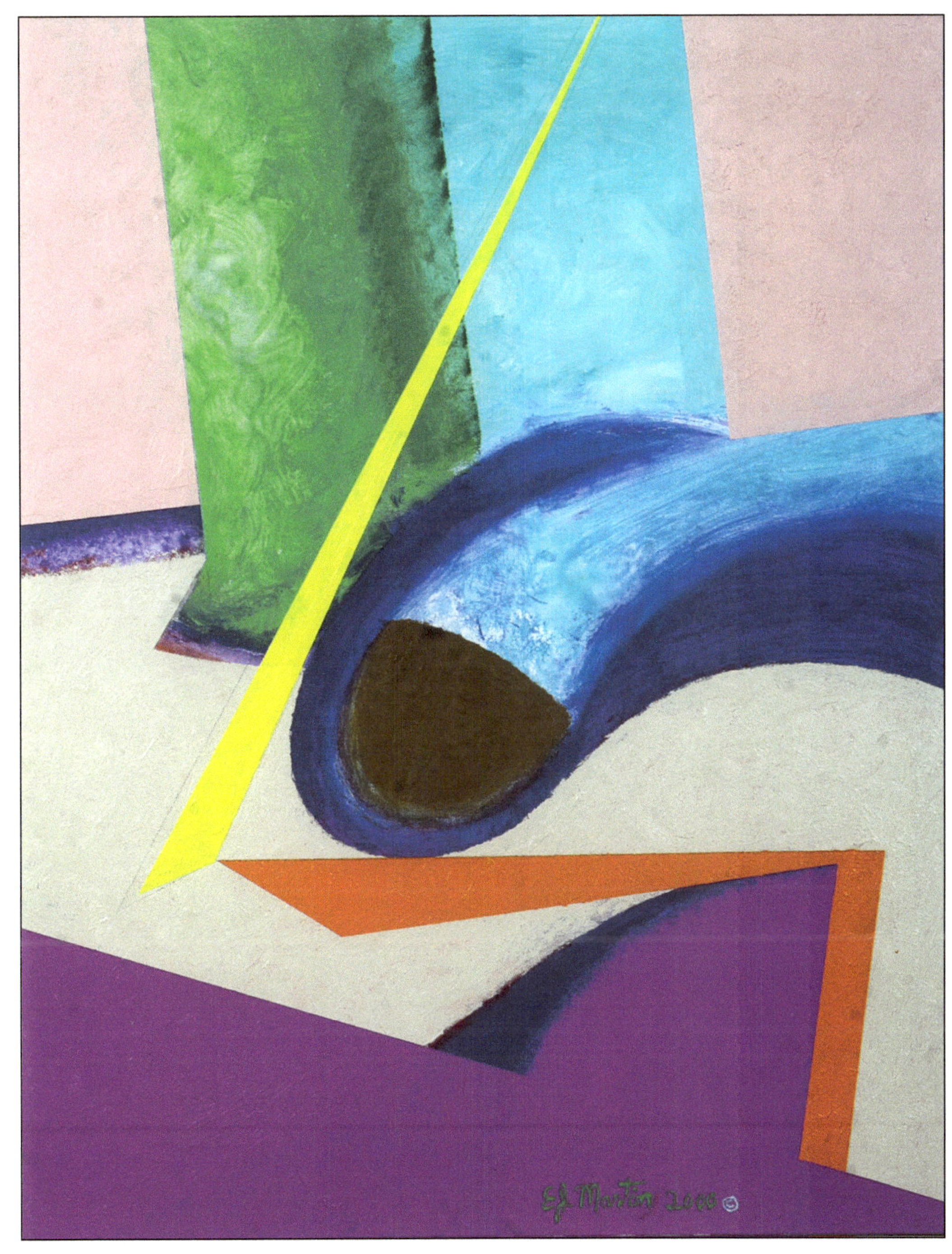
EJ Martin 2000 ©

Untitled, 2000, acrylic on canvas (at right, close-up above), 30x24"

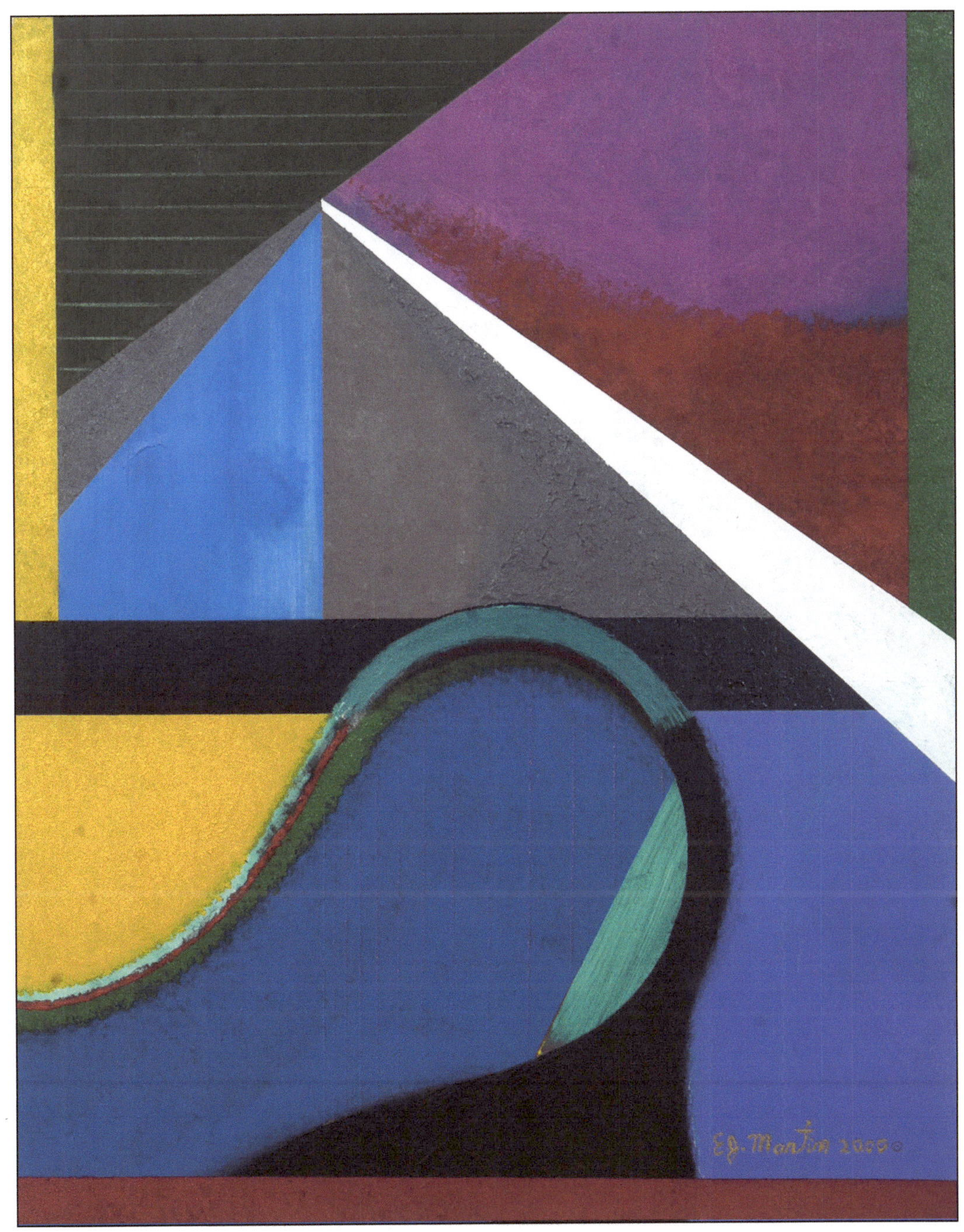

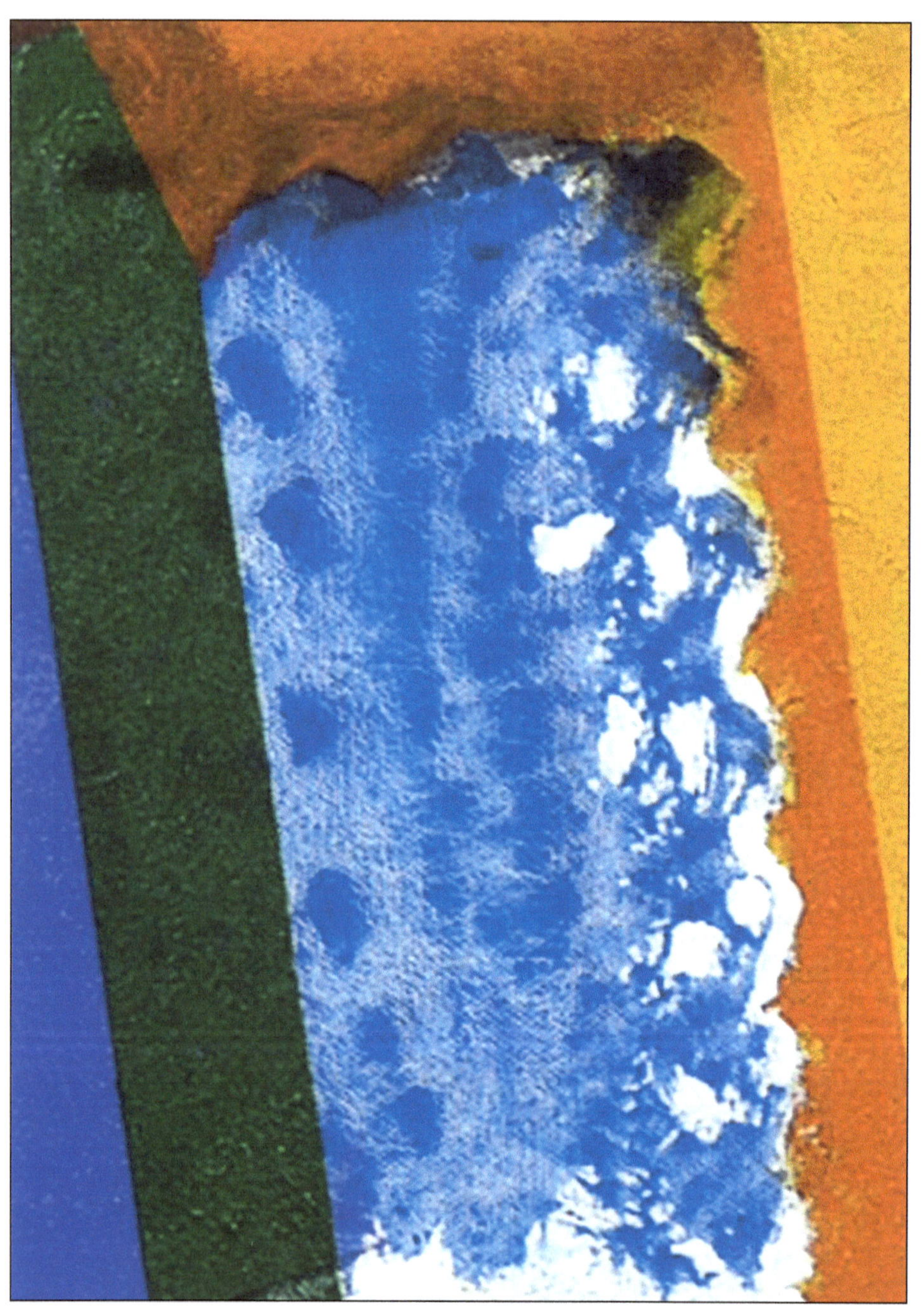

Untitled, 2000, acrylic on canvas (at right, close-up above), 30x24"

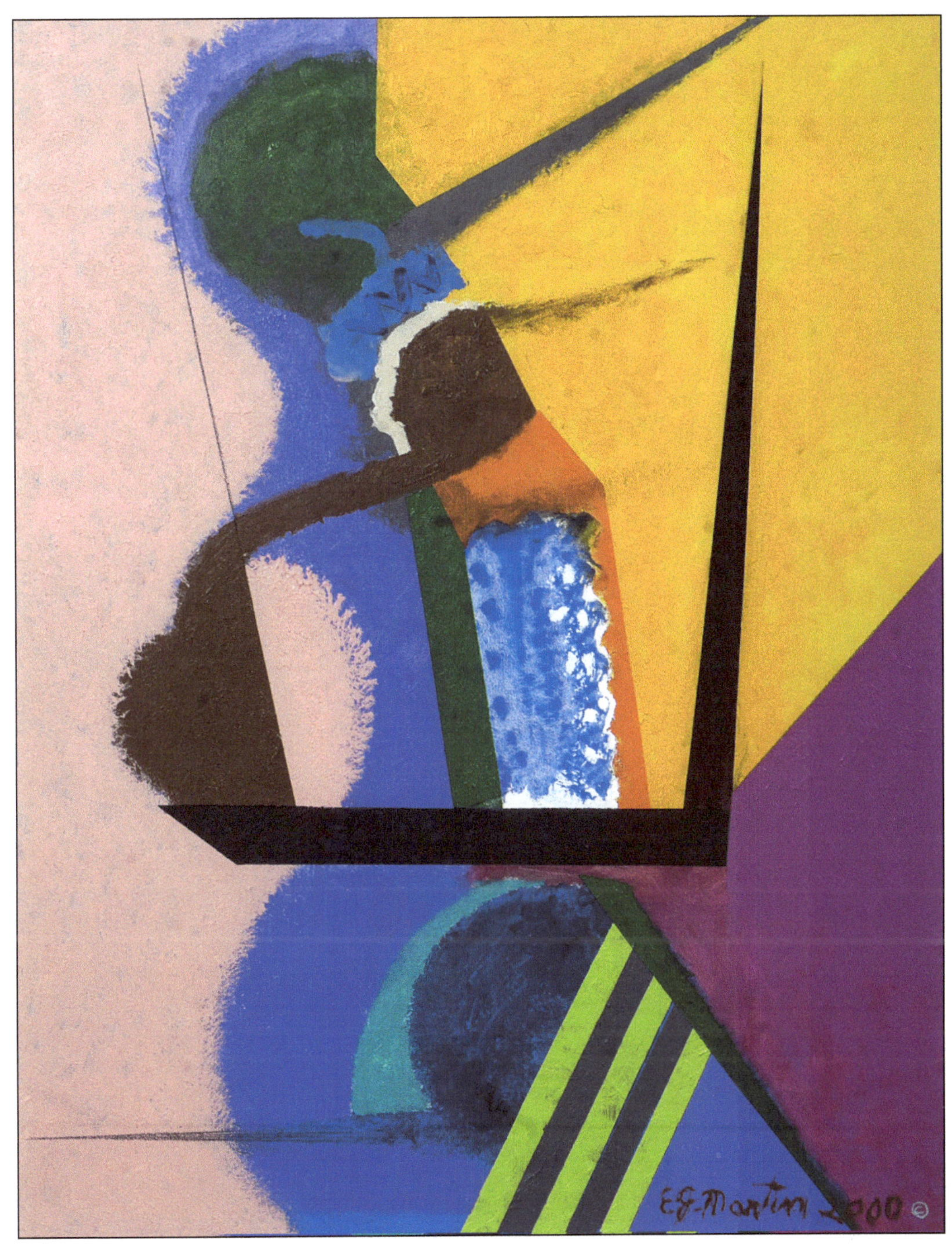
E.G. Martin 2000 ©

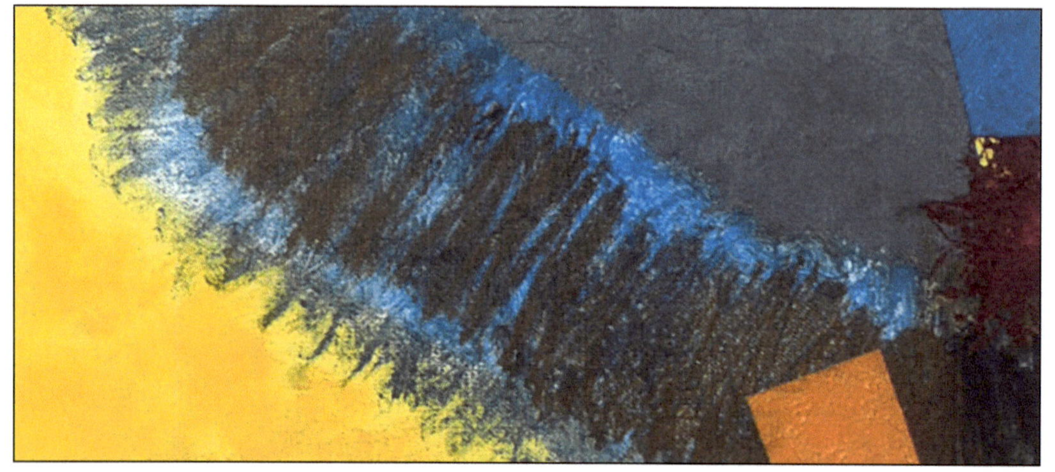

Untitled, 2000, acrylic on canvas (at right, close-up above), 30x24"

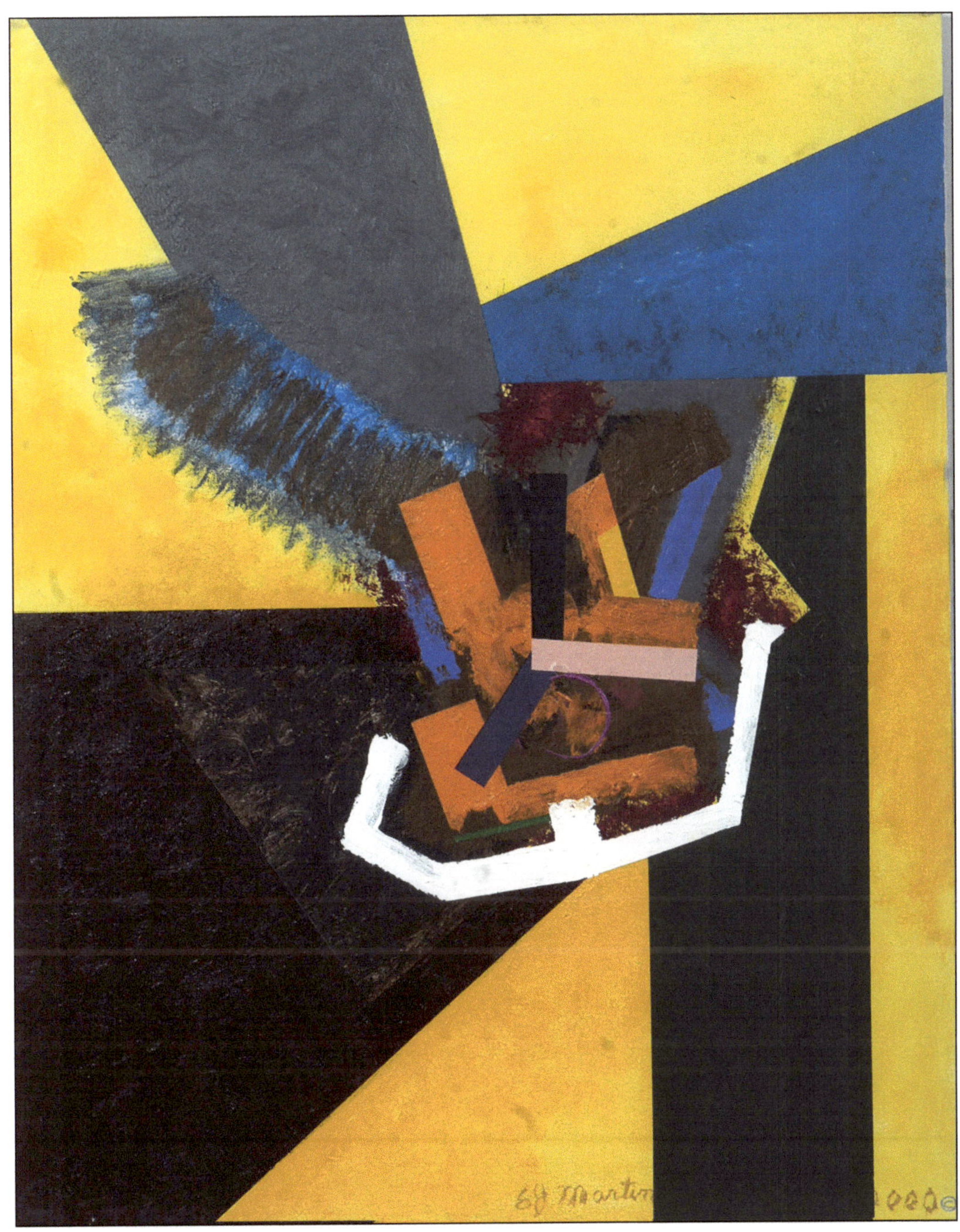

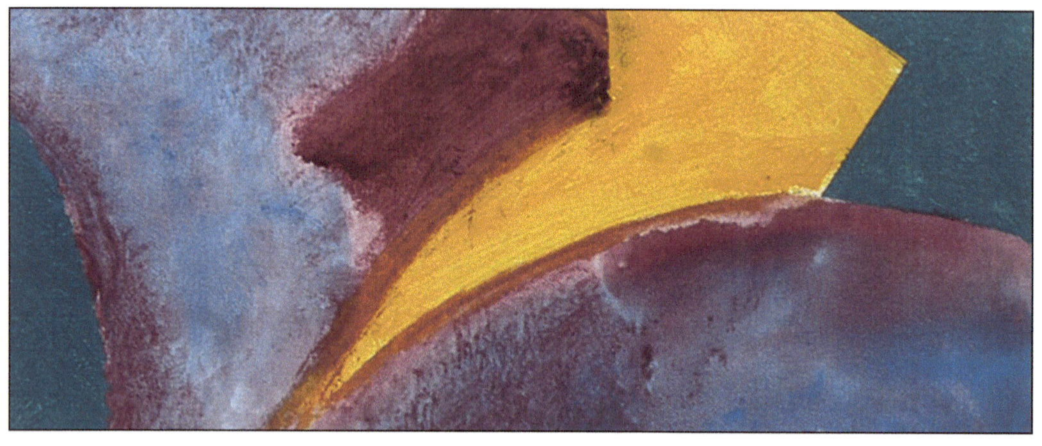

Untitled, 2000, acrylic on canvas (at right, close-up above), 30x24"

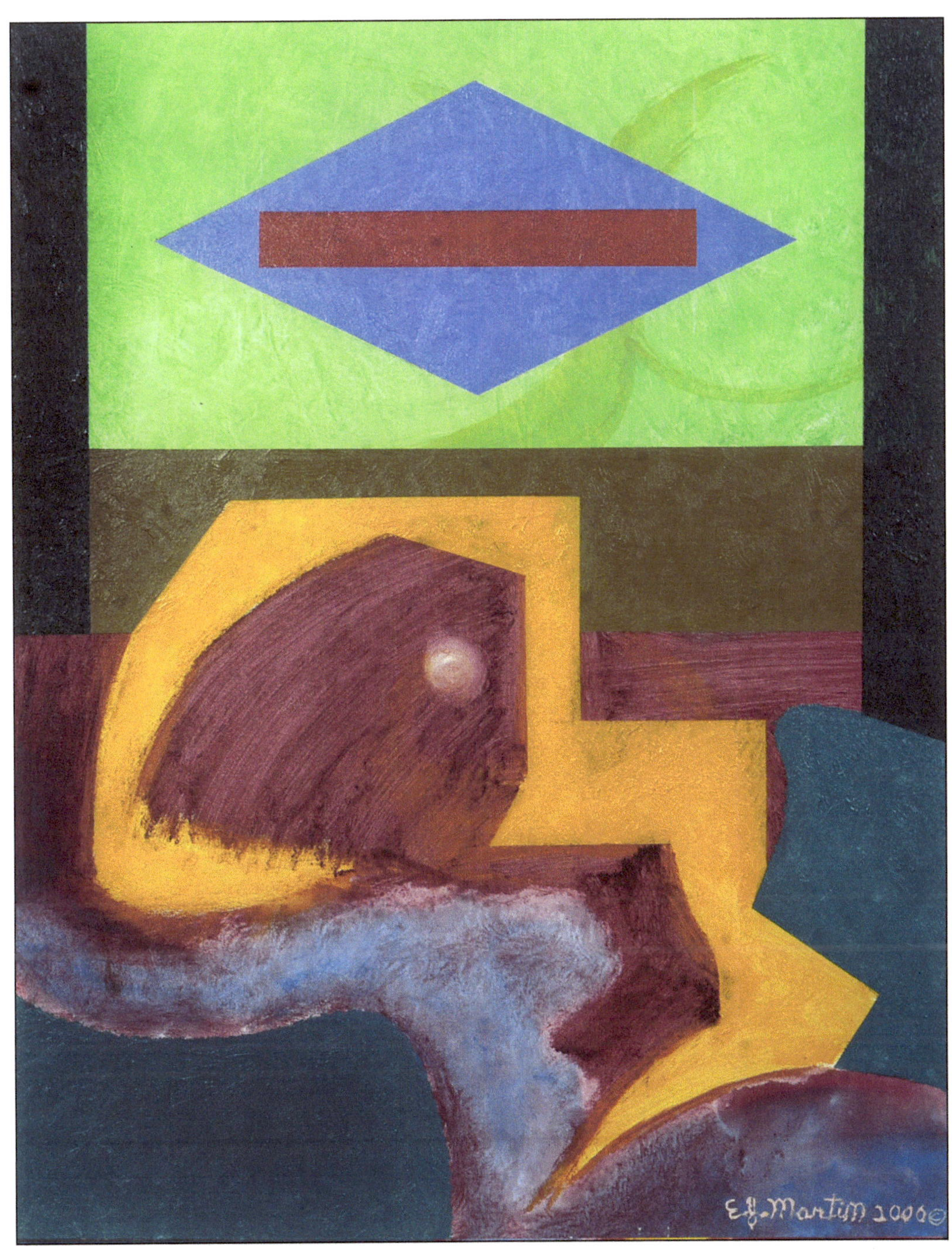

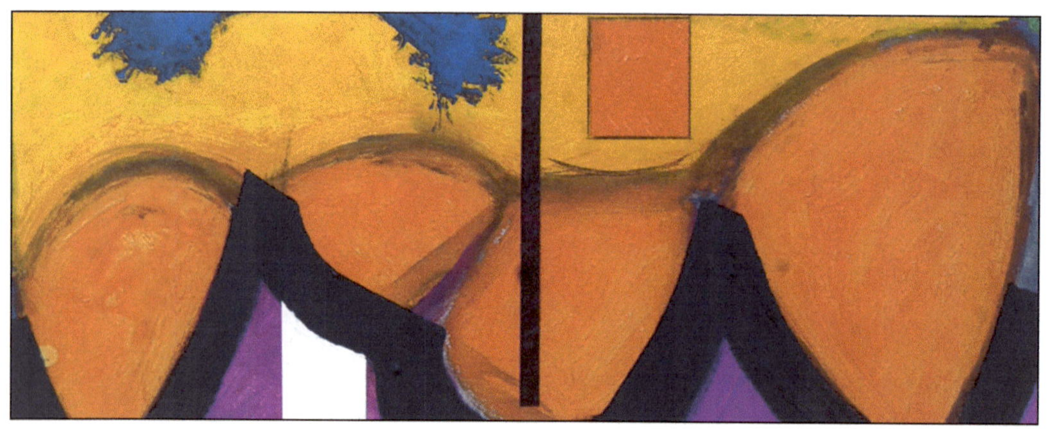

Untitled, 2000, acrylic on canvas (at right, close-up above), 30x24"

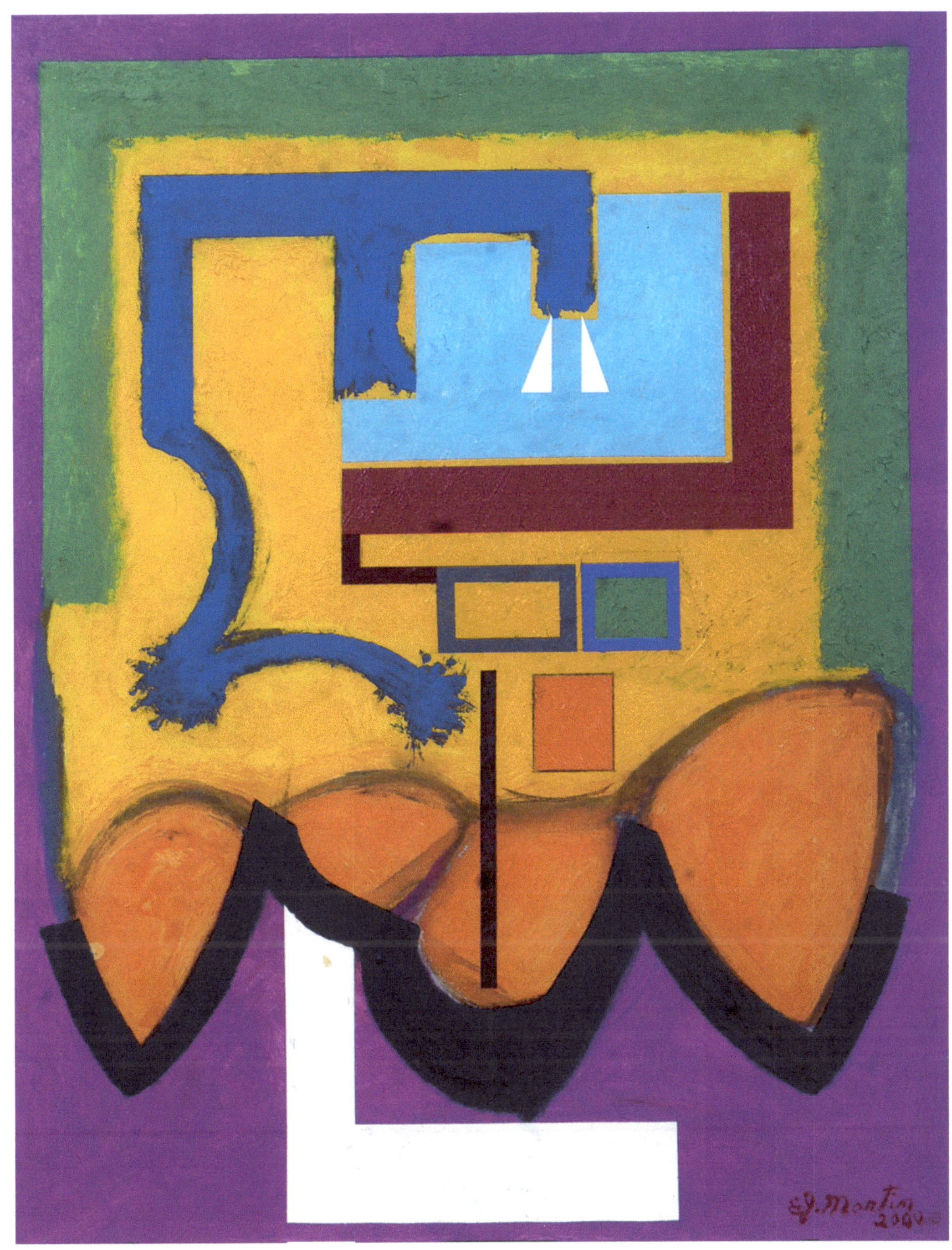
E.J. Martin
2000

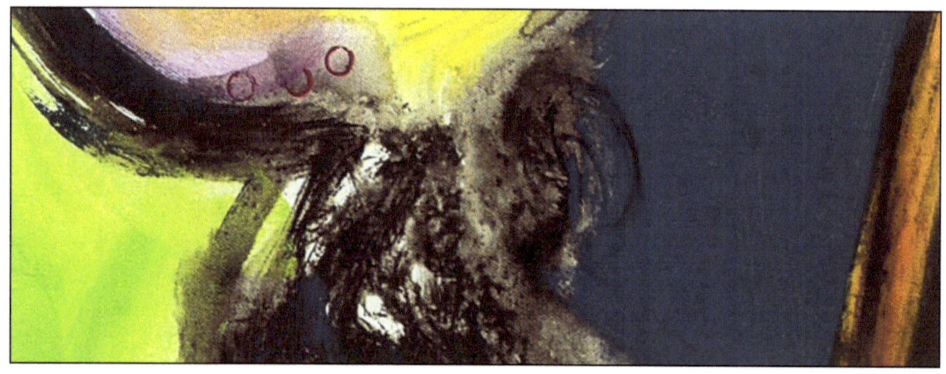

Untitled, 2000, acrylic on canvas (at right, close-up above), 30x24"

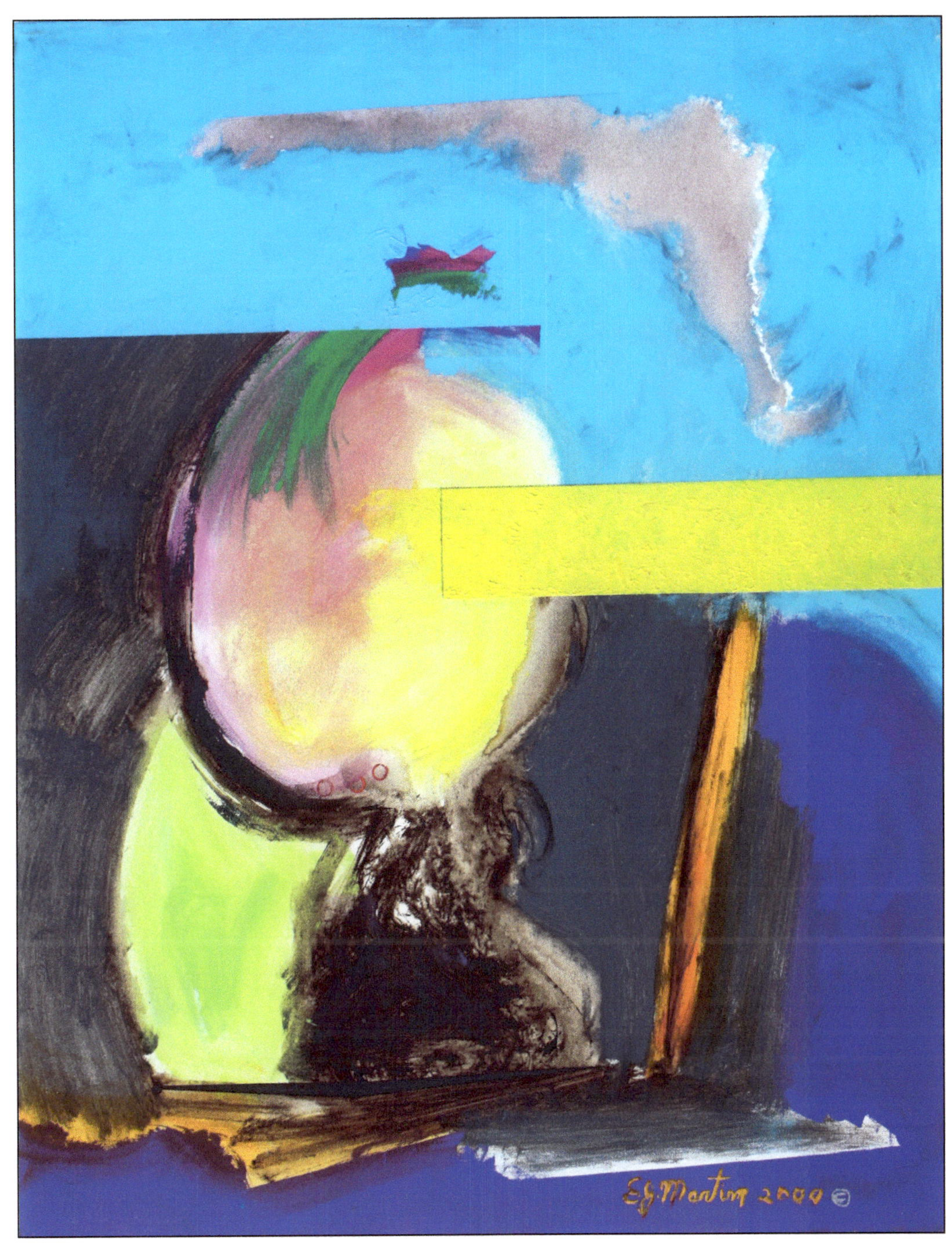
E.J. Martin 2000 ©

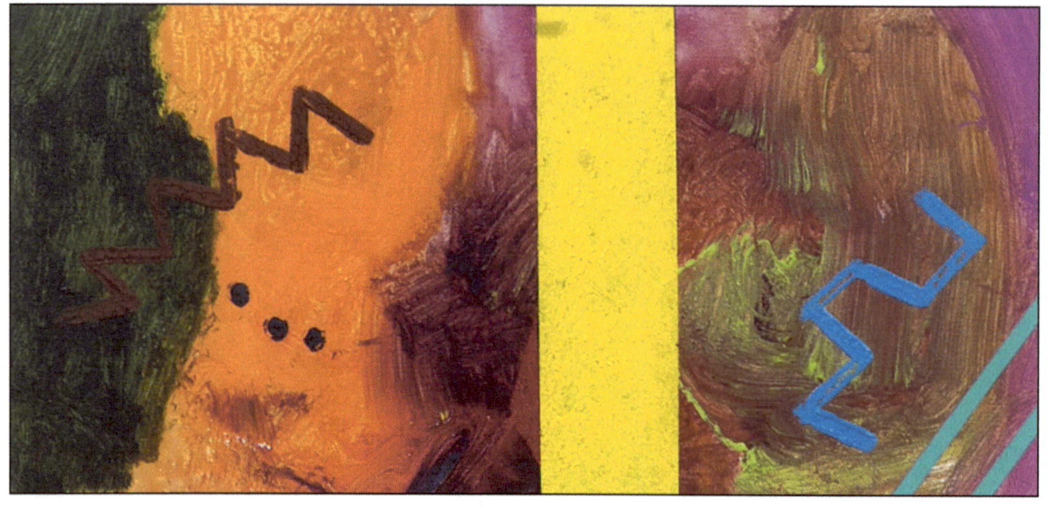

Untitled, 2000, acrylic on canvas (at right, close-up above), 30x24"

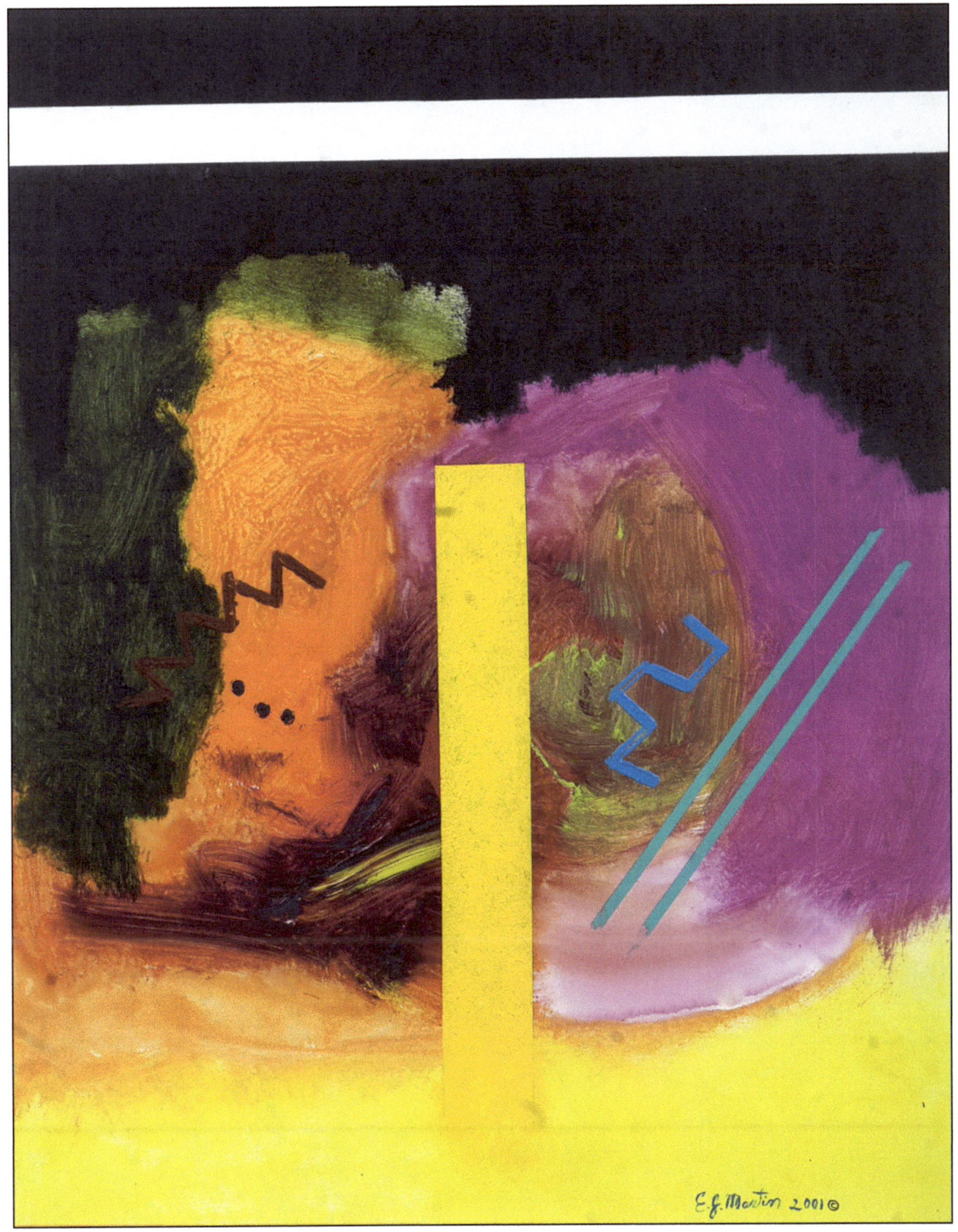
E.J. Martin 2001©

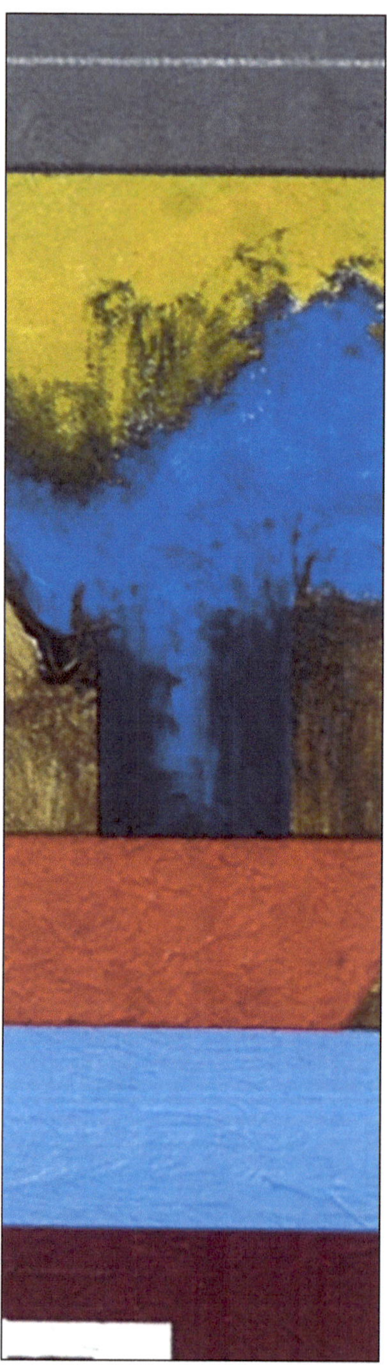

Untitled, 2000, acrylic on canvas (at right, close-up above), 30x24"

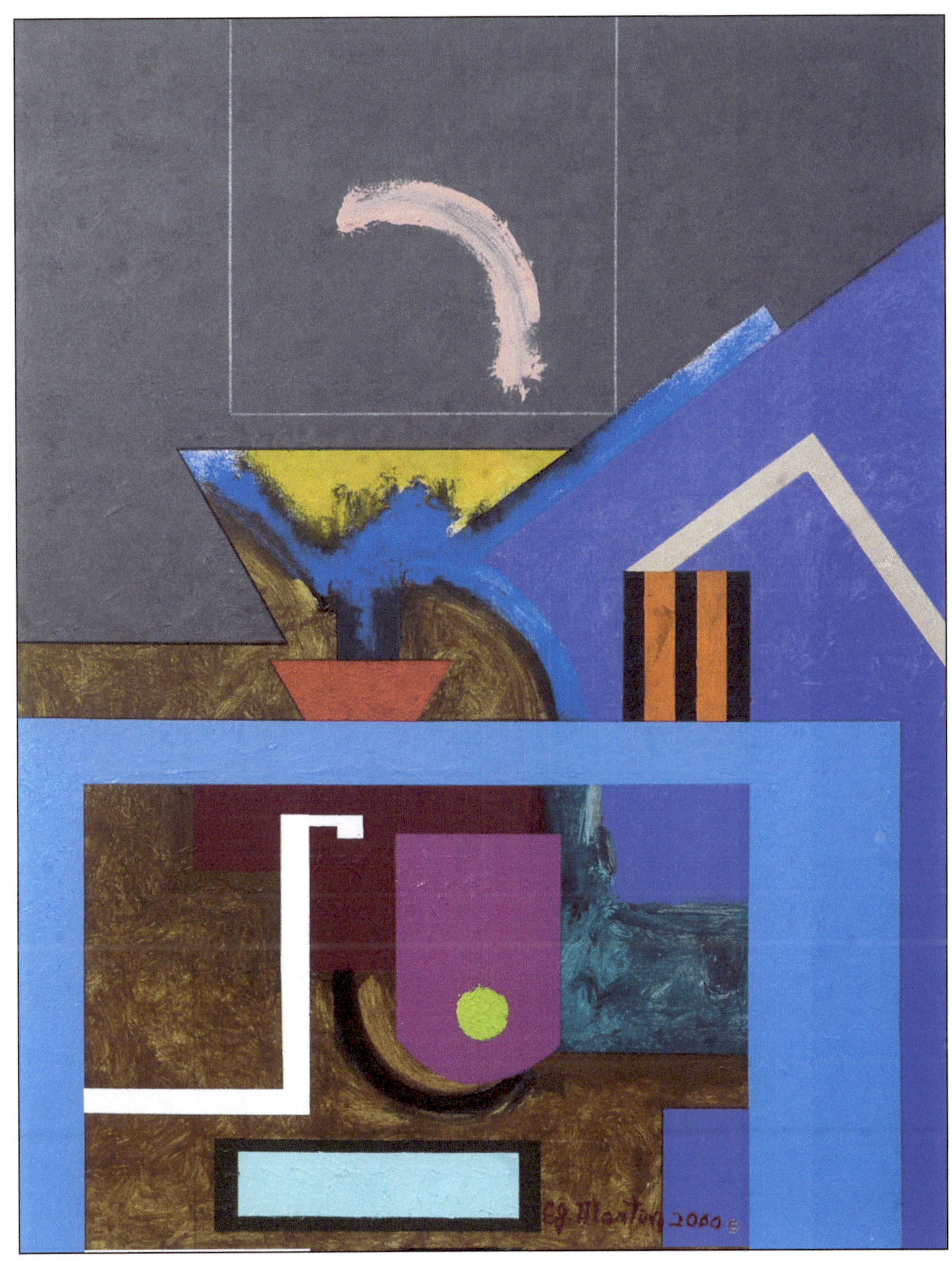

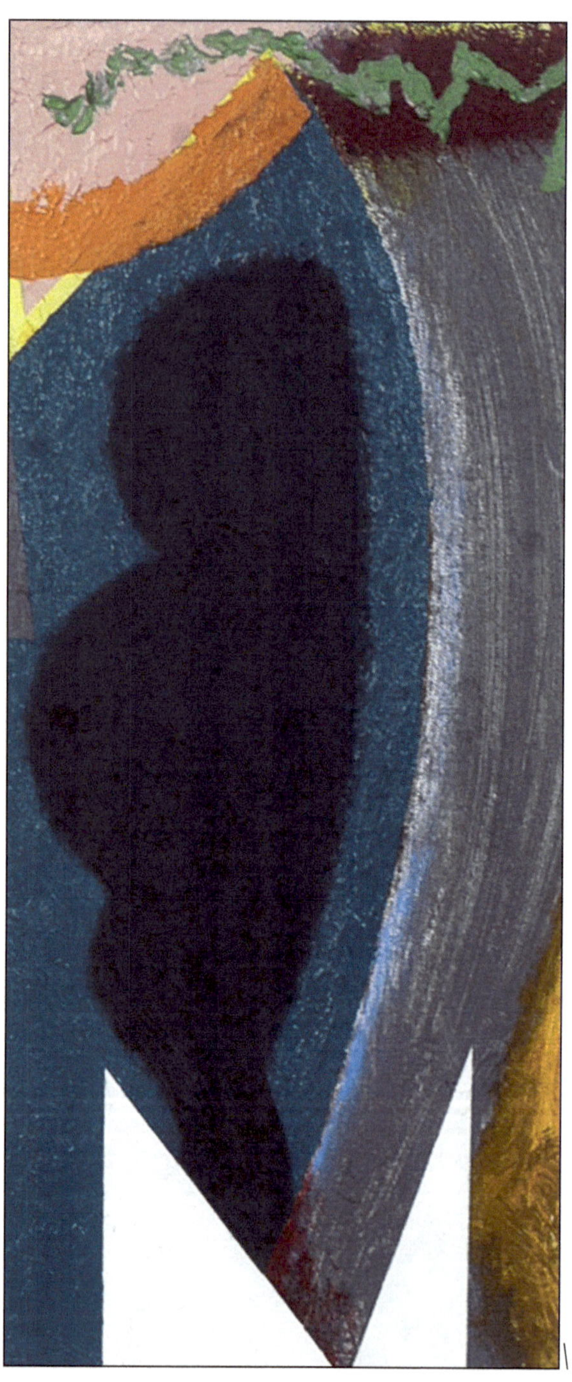

Untitled, 2000, acrylic on canvas (at right, close-up above), 30x24"

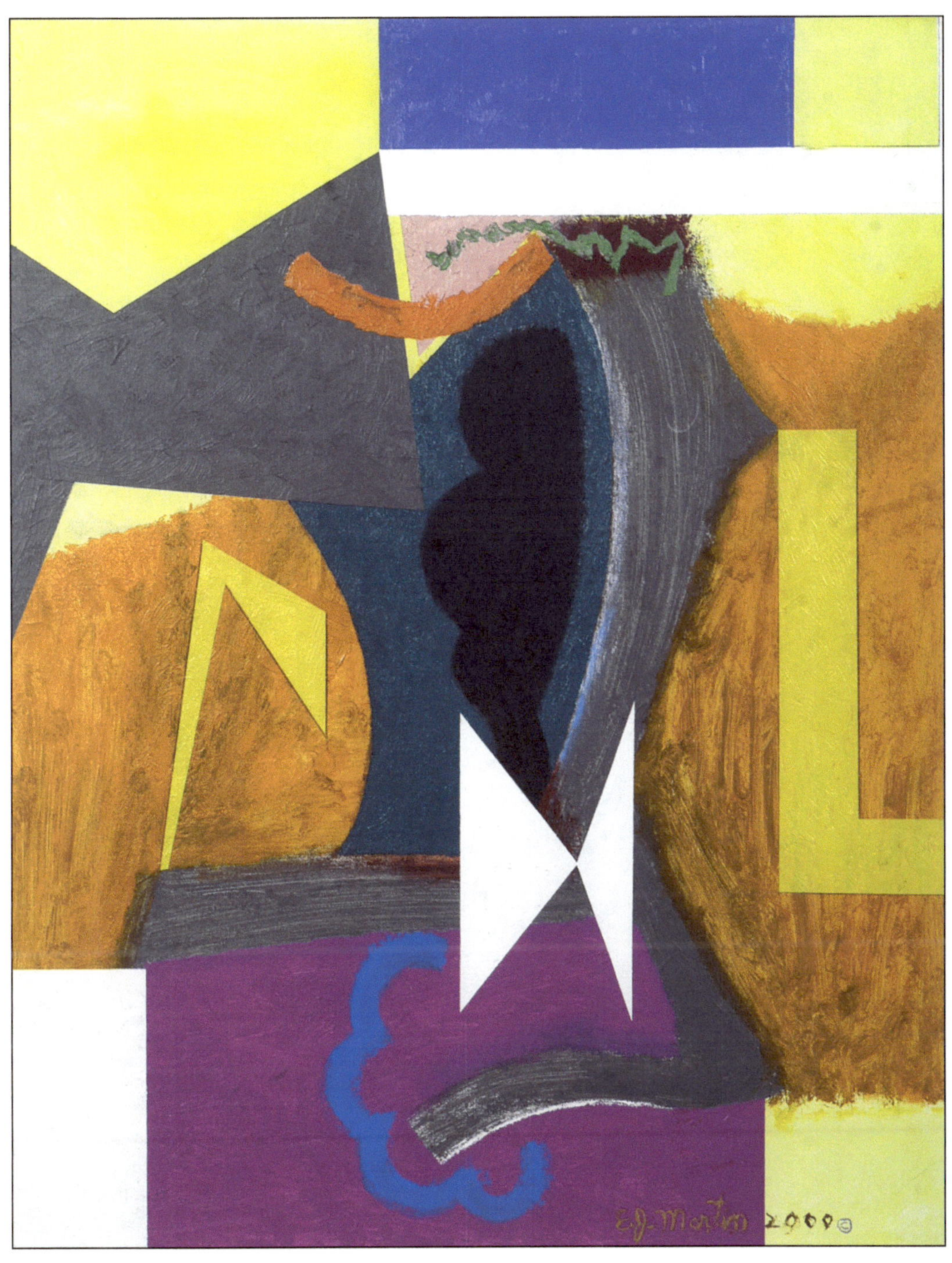
E.J. Martin 2000©

Untitled, 2000, acrylic on canvas (at right, close-up above), 30x24"

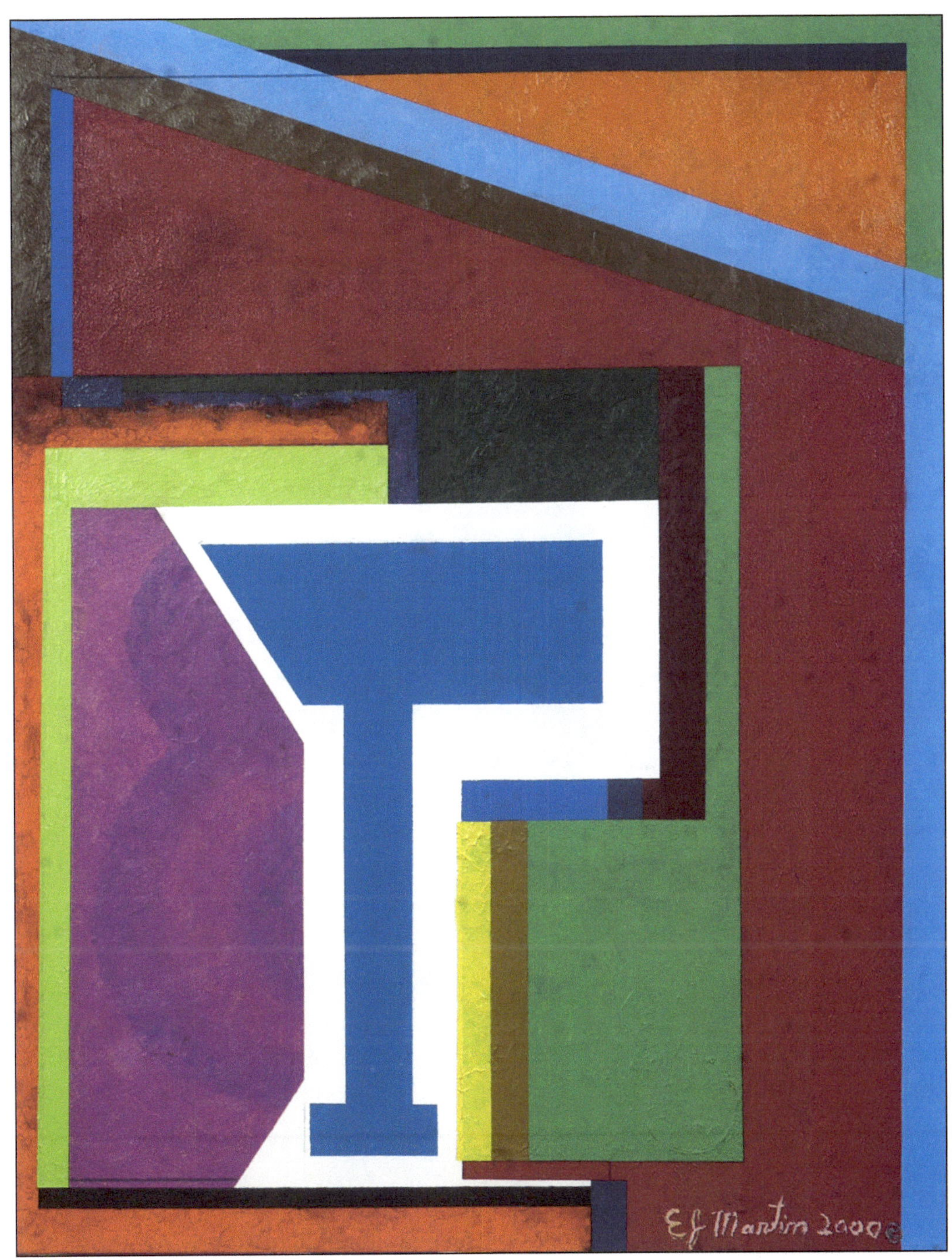
Ef Martin 2000

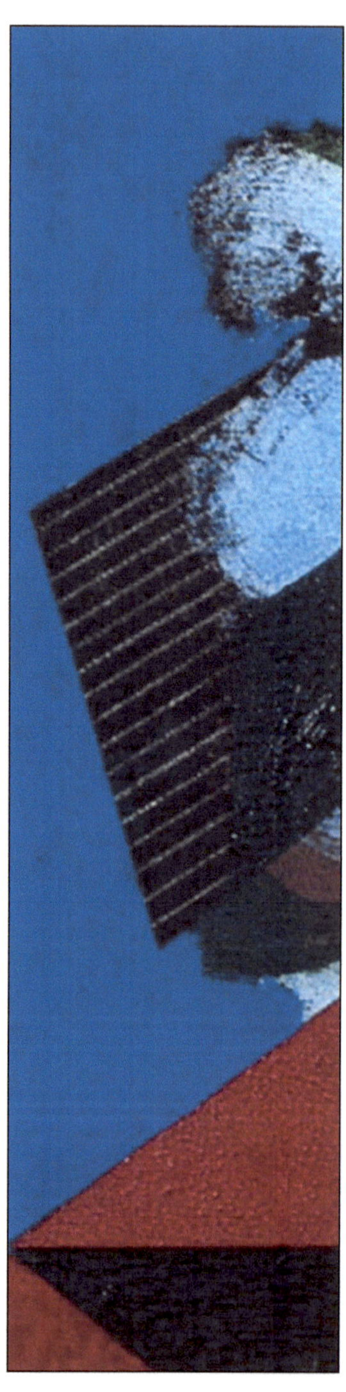

Untitled, 2000, acrylic on canvas (at right, close-up above), 30x24"

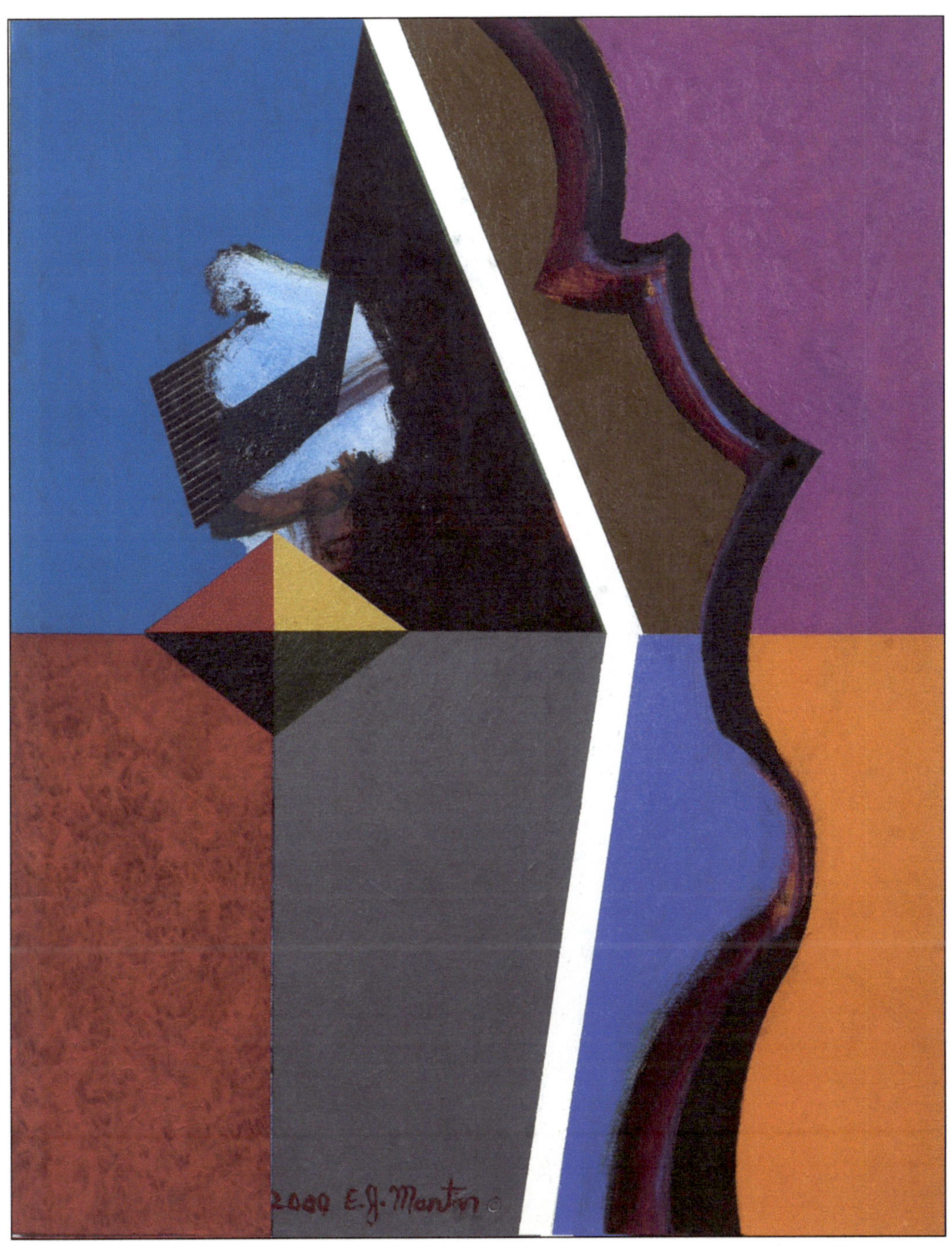
2000 E.J. Martin ©

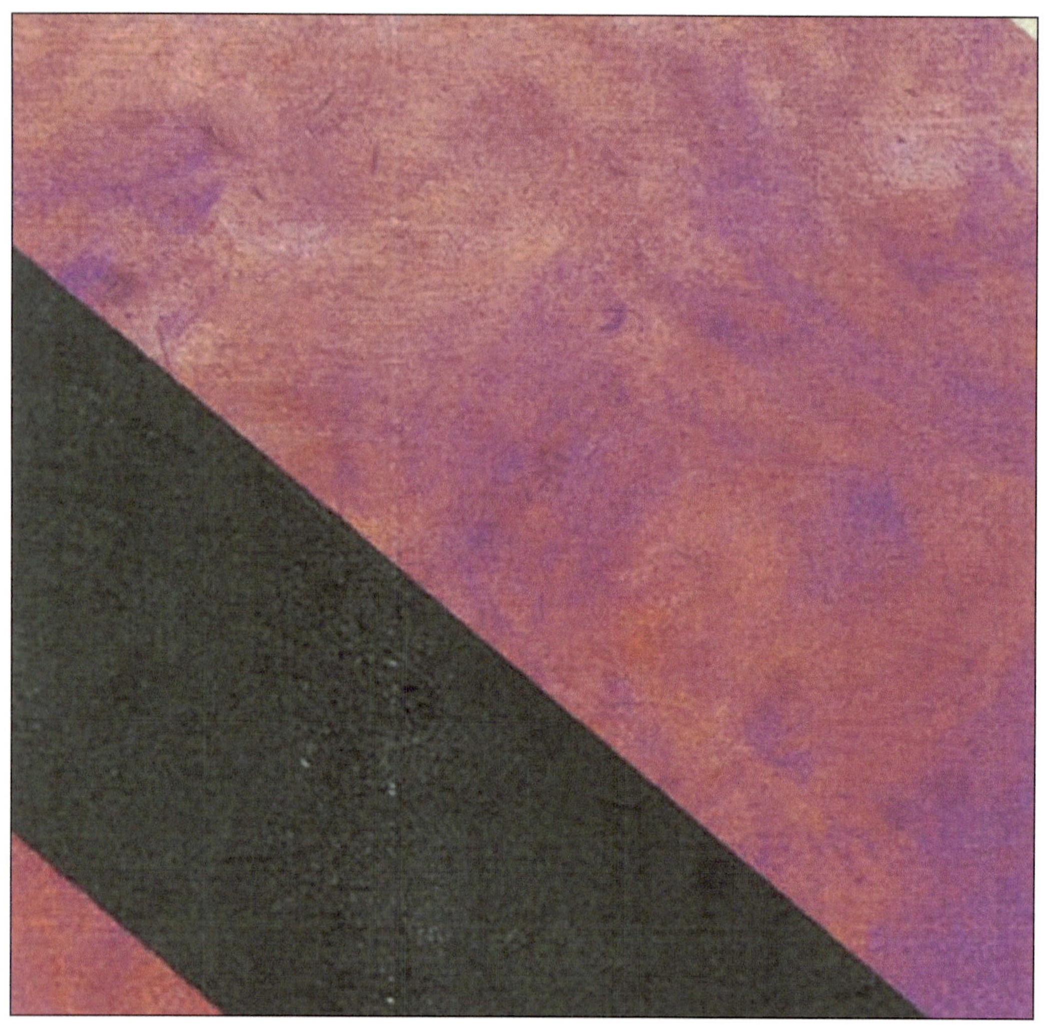

Untitled, 2000, acrylic on canvas (at right, close-up above), 30x24"

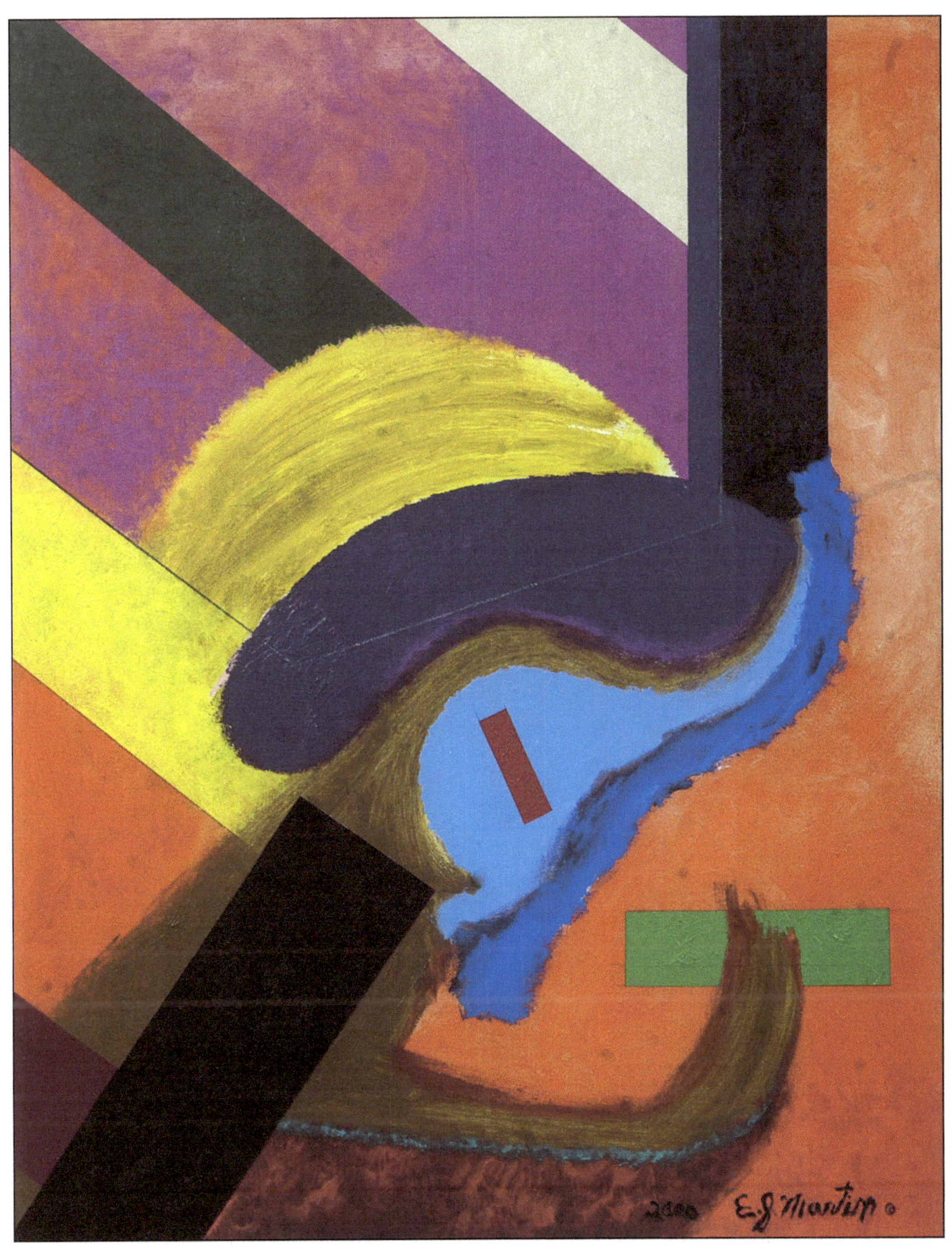
2000 E.J. Martin

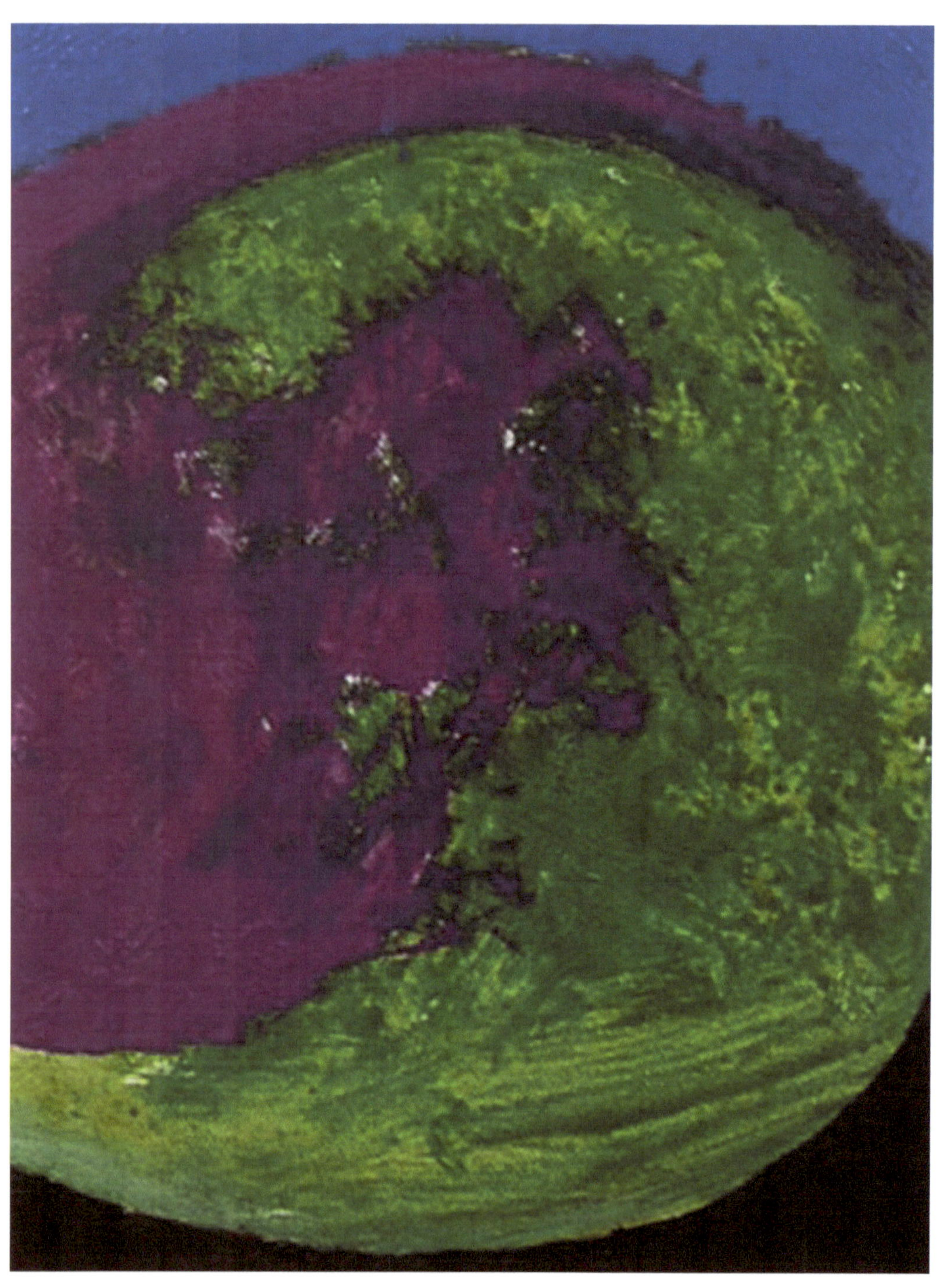

Untitled, 2000, acrylic on canvas (at right, close-up above), 30x24"

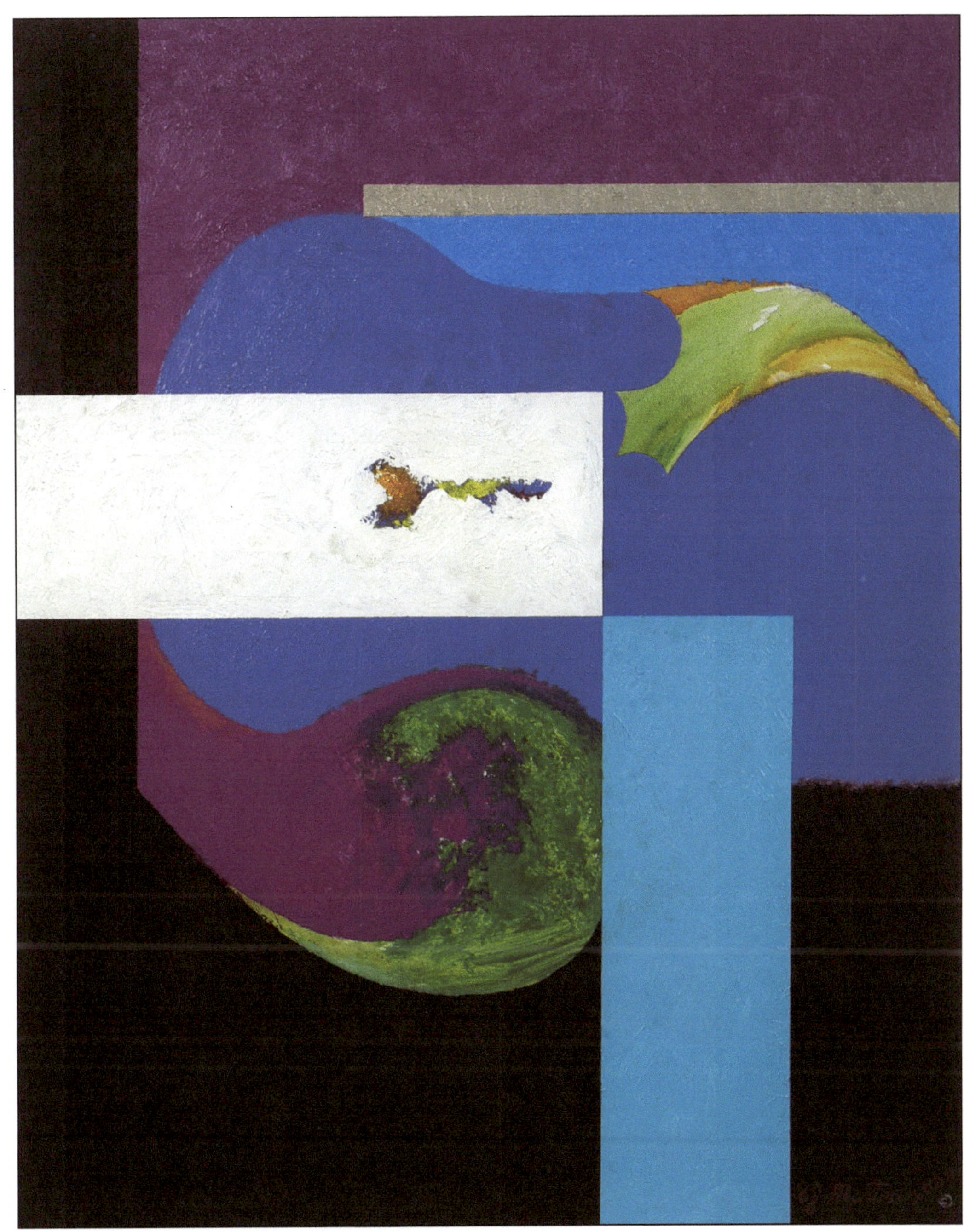

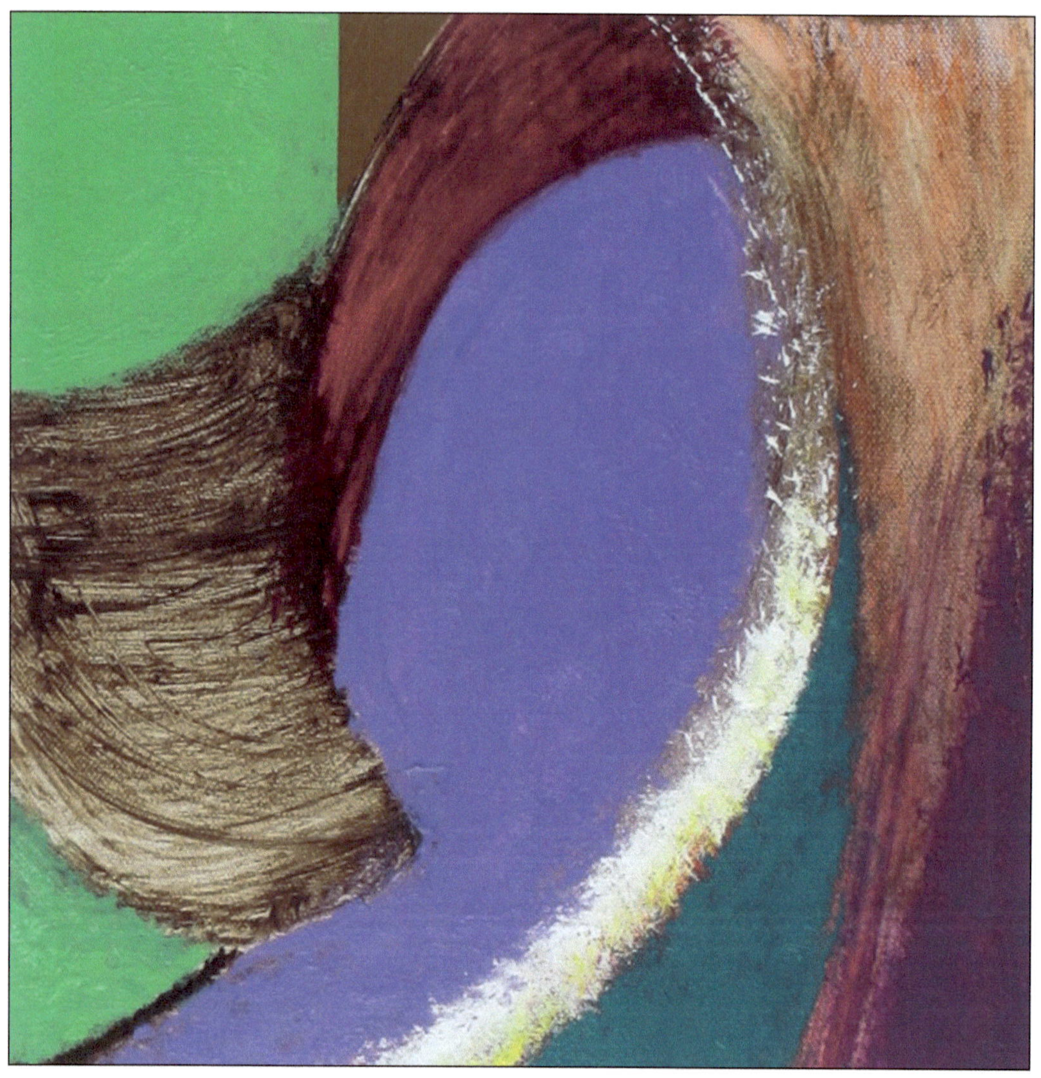

Untitled, 2000, acrylic on canvas (at right, close-up above), 30x24"

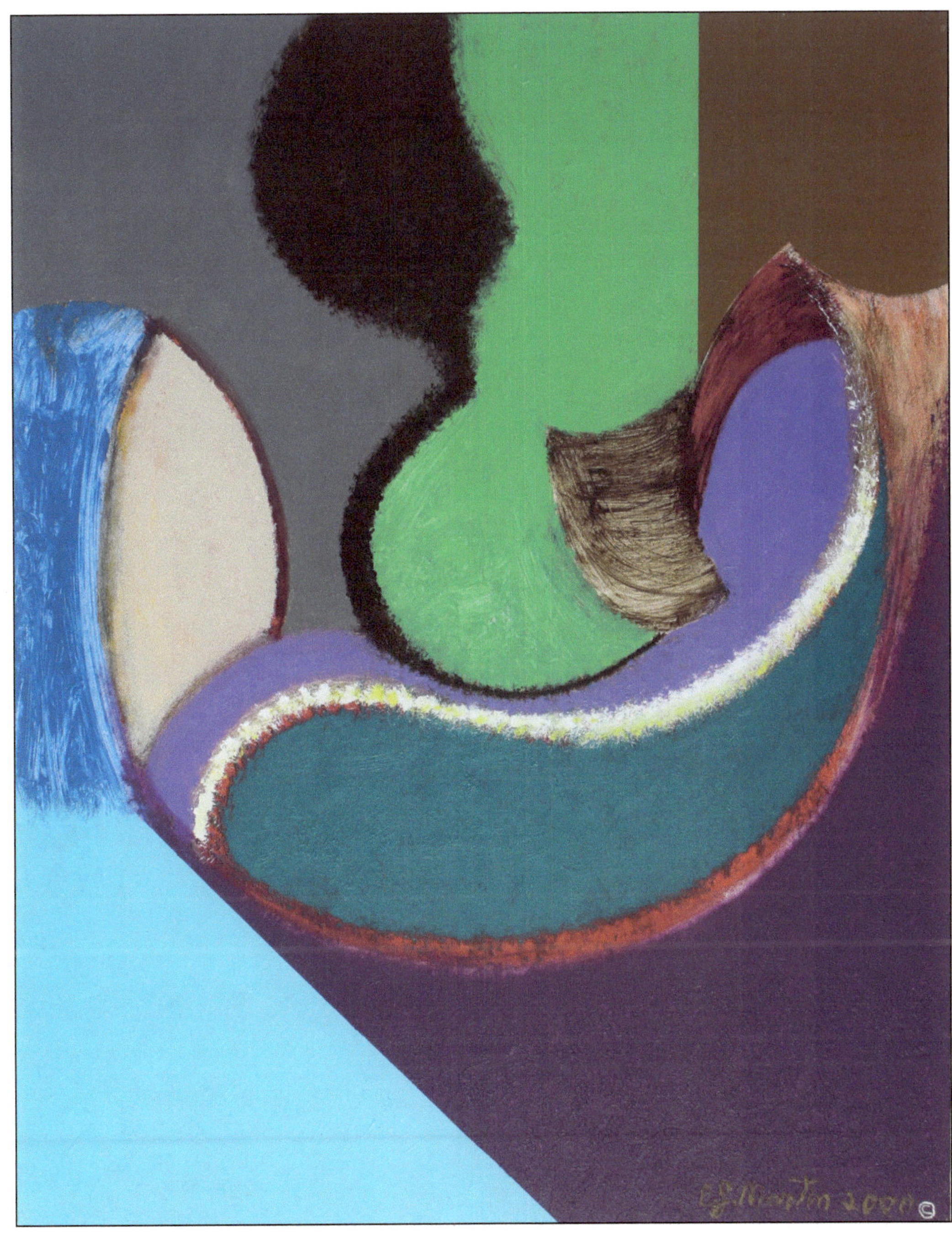

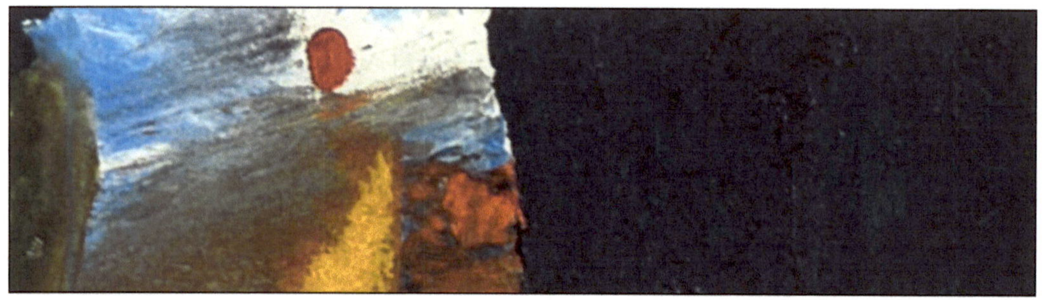

Untitled, 2000, acrylic on canvas (at right, close-up above), 30x24"

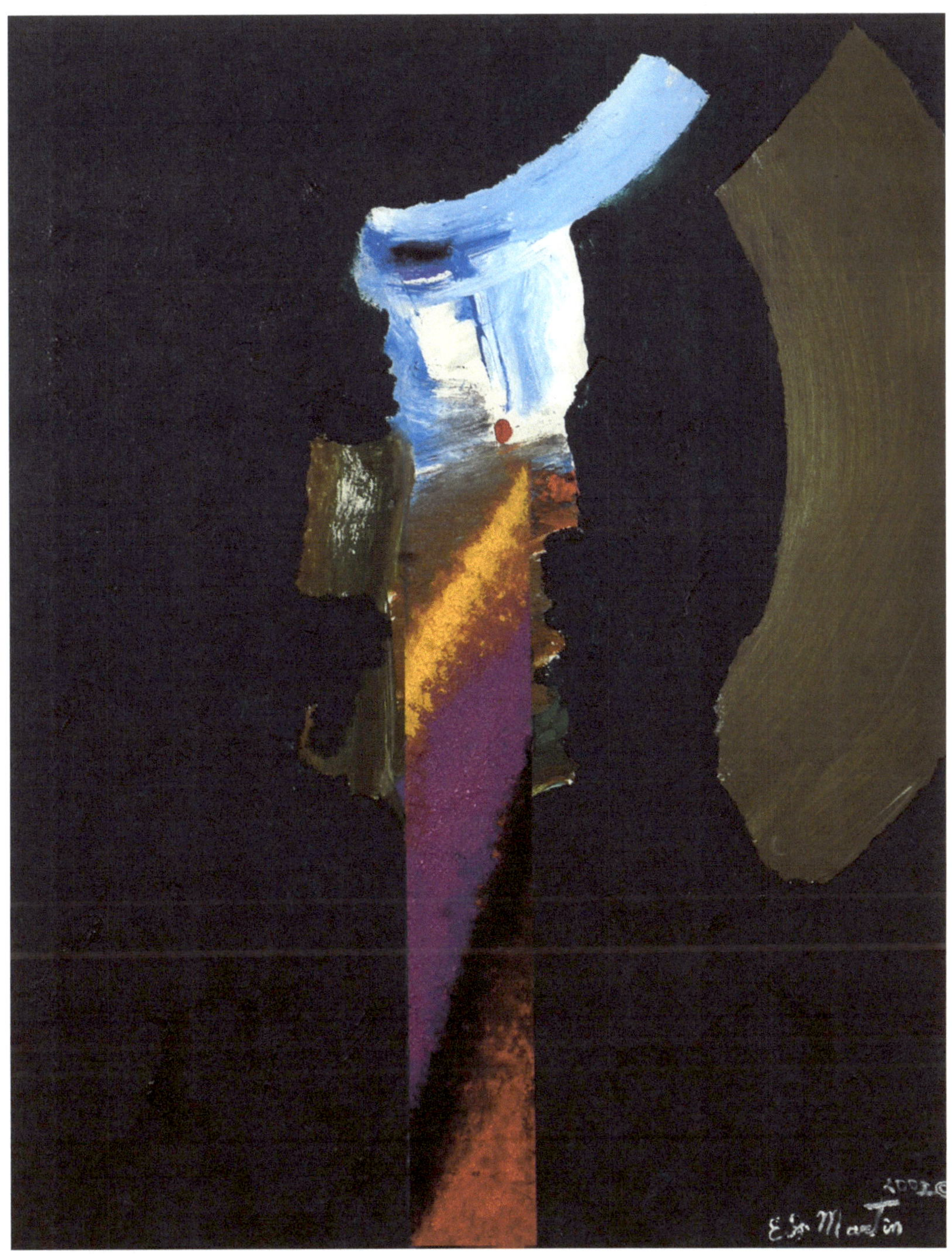

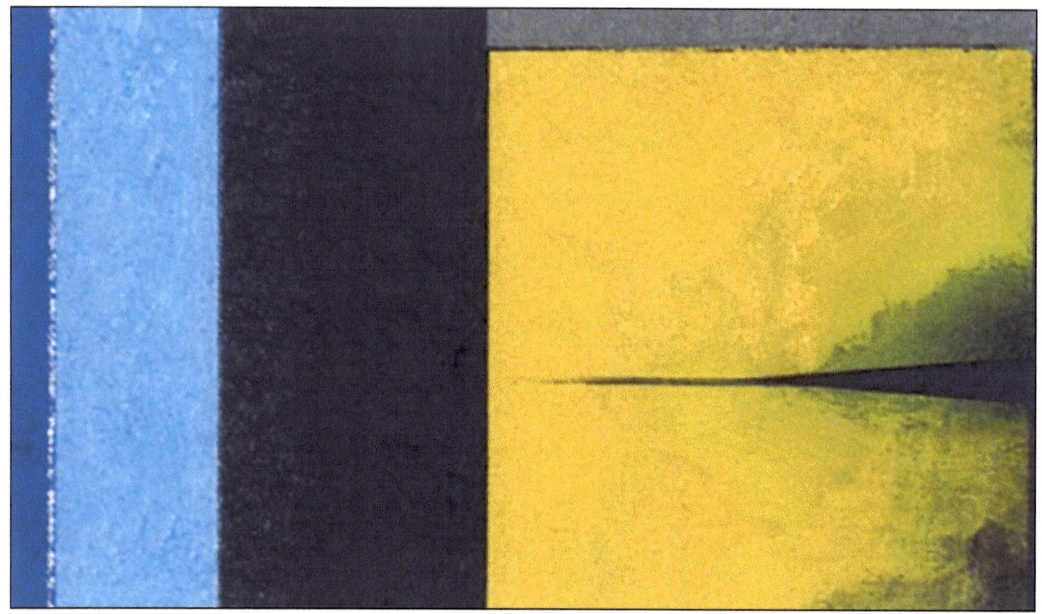

Untitled, 2000, acrylic on canvas (at right, close-up above), 30x24"

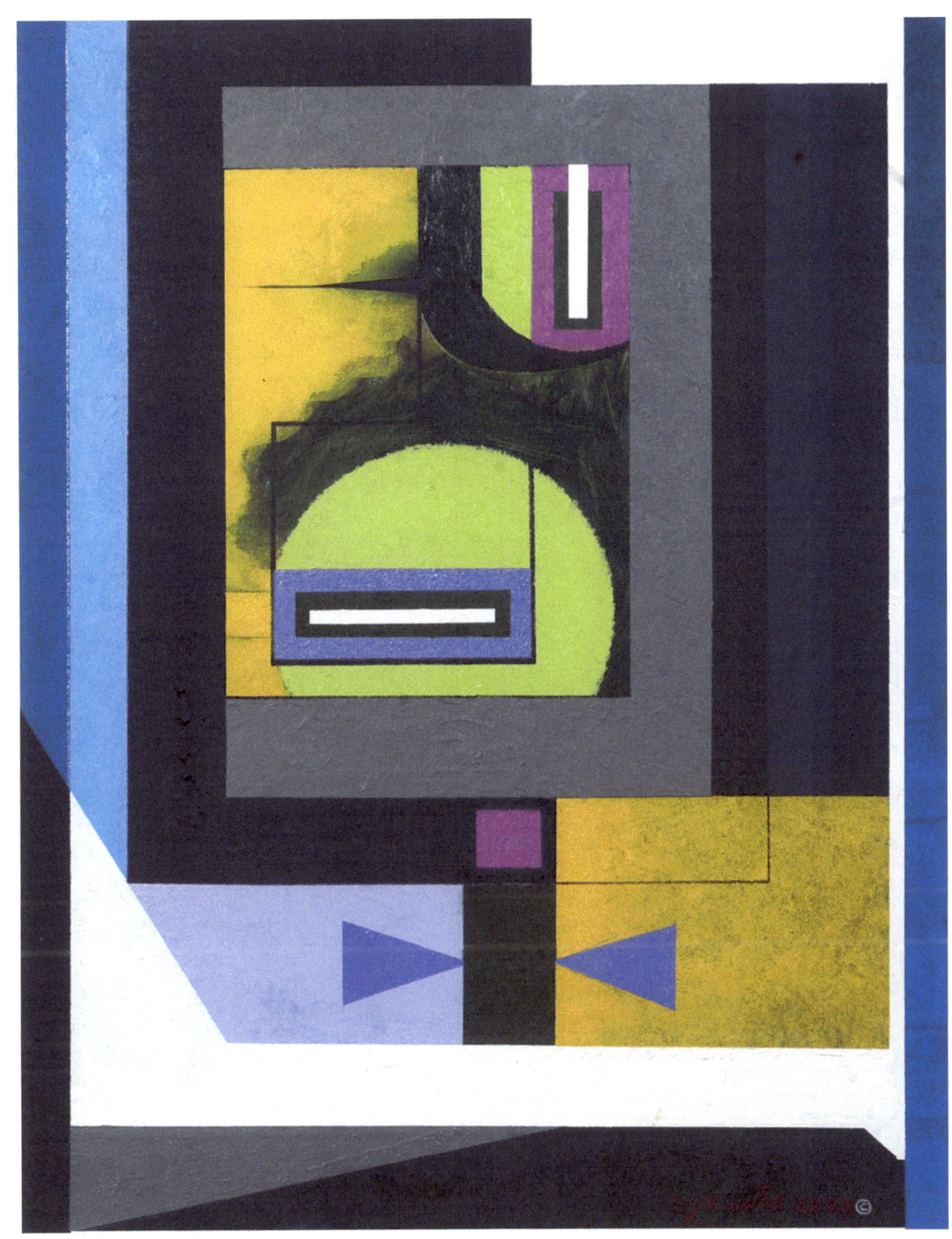

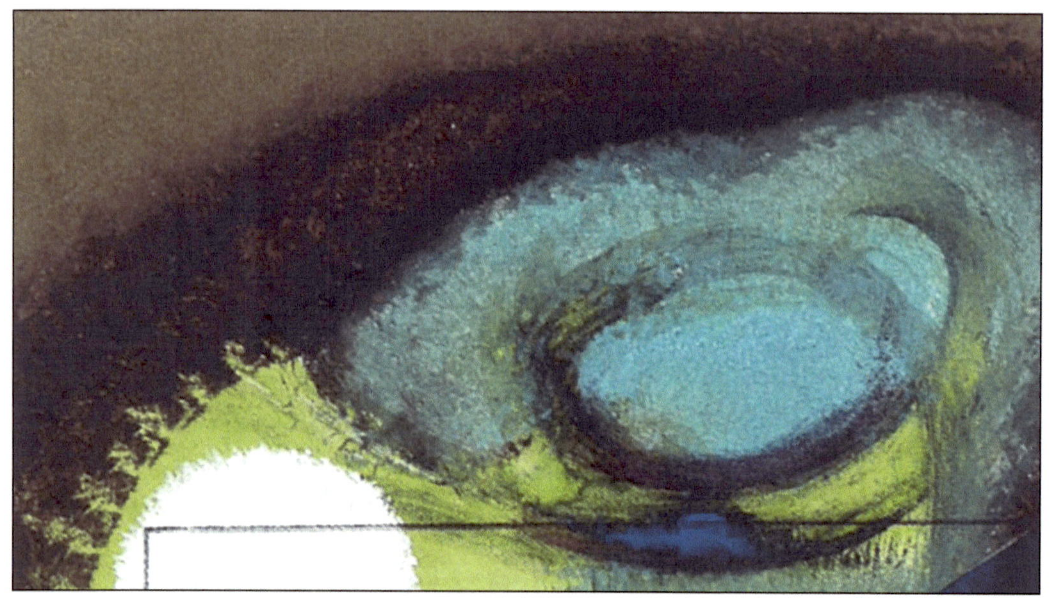

Mean and Green, 2000, acrylic on canvas (at right, close-up above), 30x24"

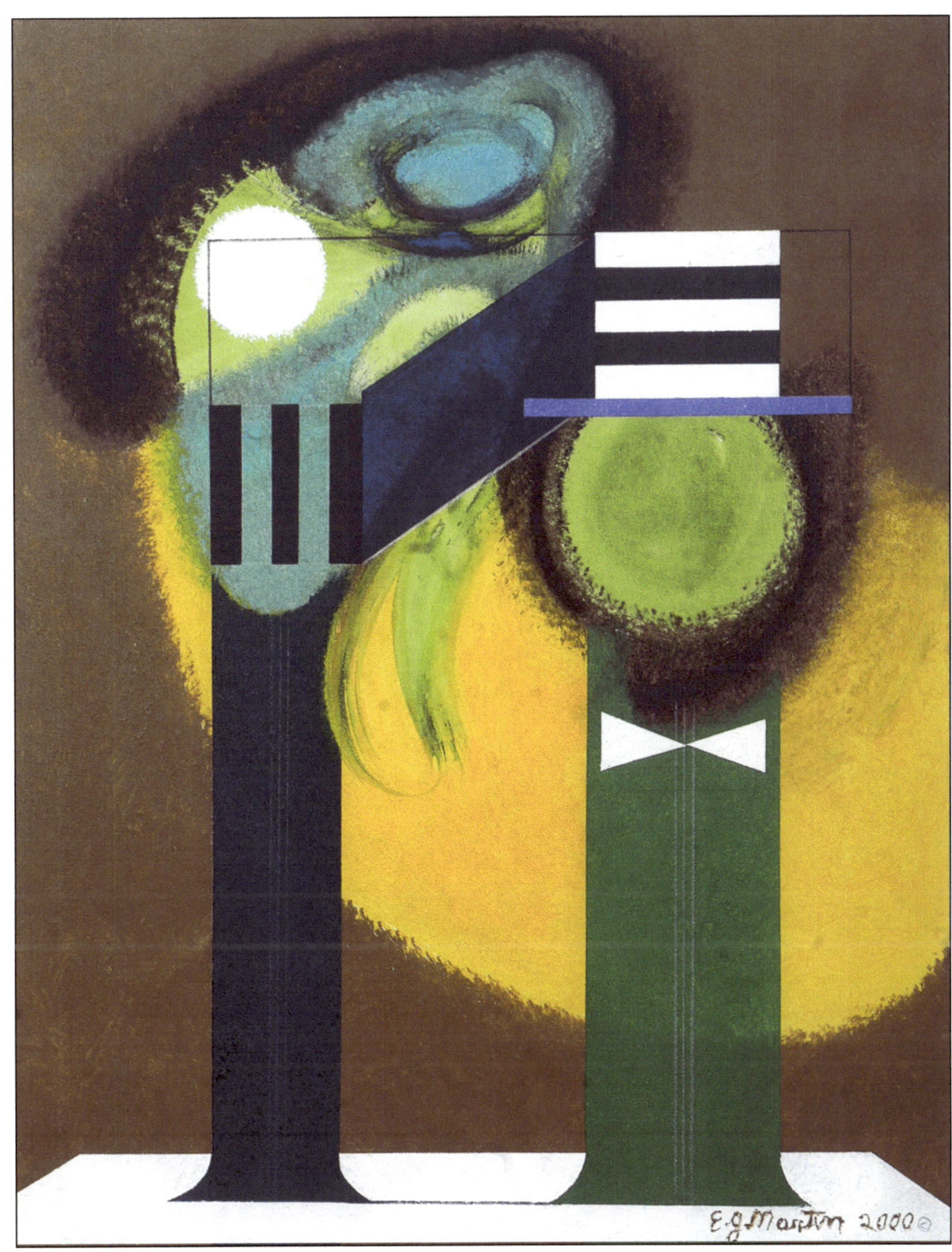
E.G.Martin 2000©

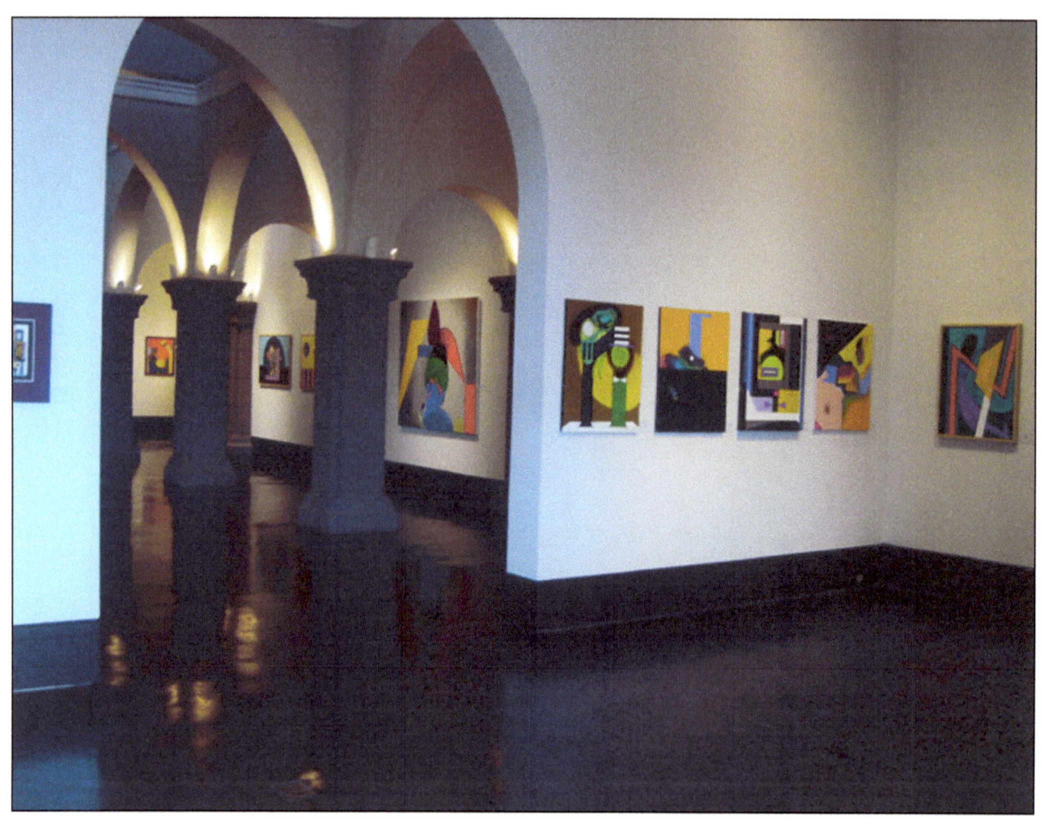

"Mean and Green" exhibited at the 2007 Eugene Martin Retrospective Exhibition at the Alexandria Museum of Art (LA)

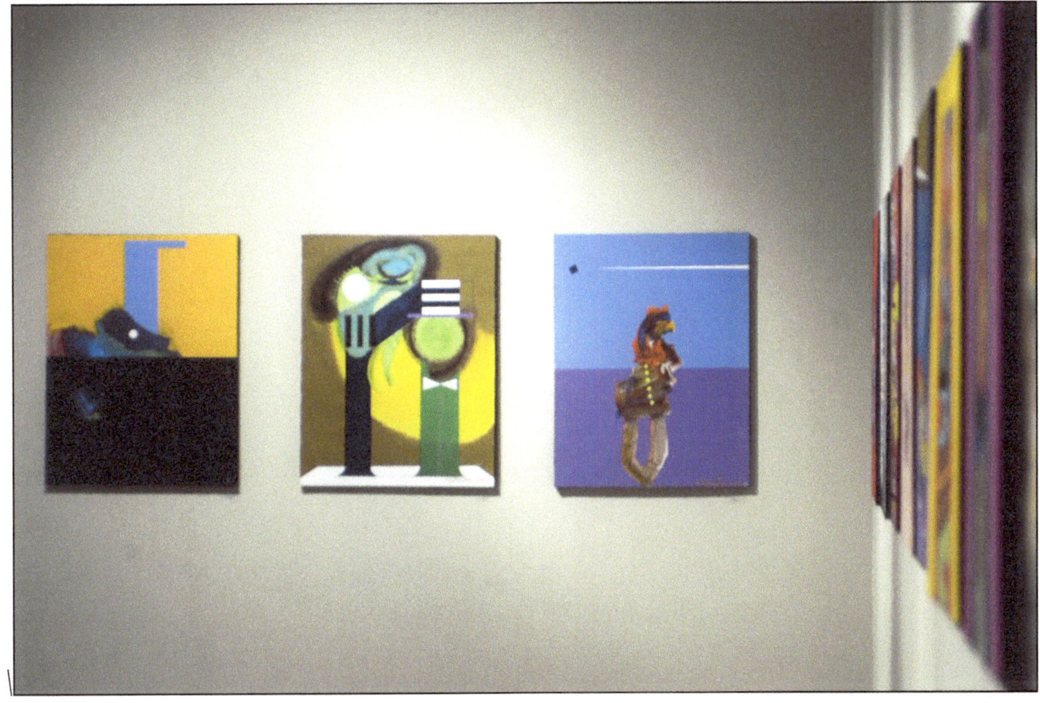

"Mean and Green" exhibited at the 2004 Eugene Martin Exhibit "The Gravy Train People and their Pets" at the Galerie Lafayette (LA)

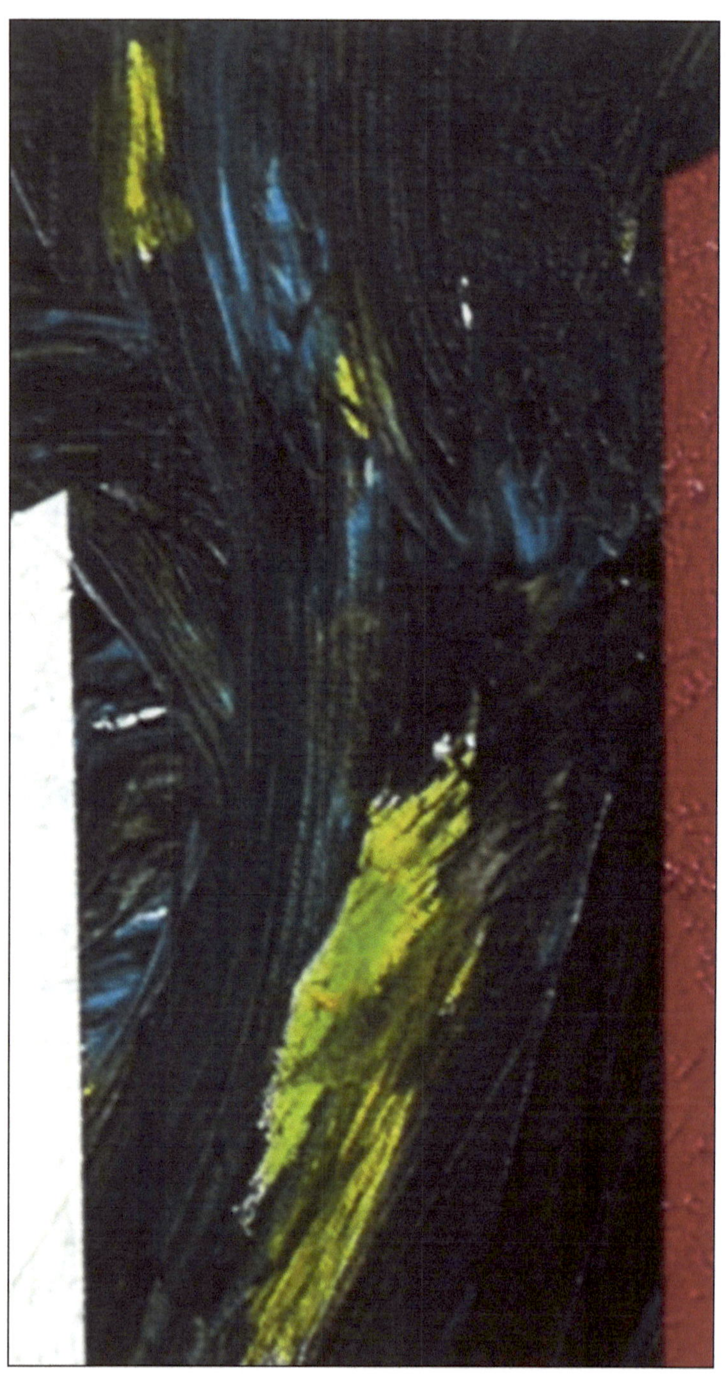

Untitled, 2000, acrylic on canvas (at right, close-up above), 30x24"

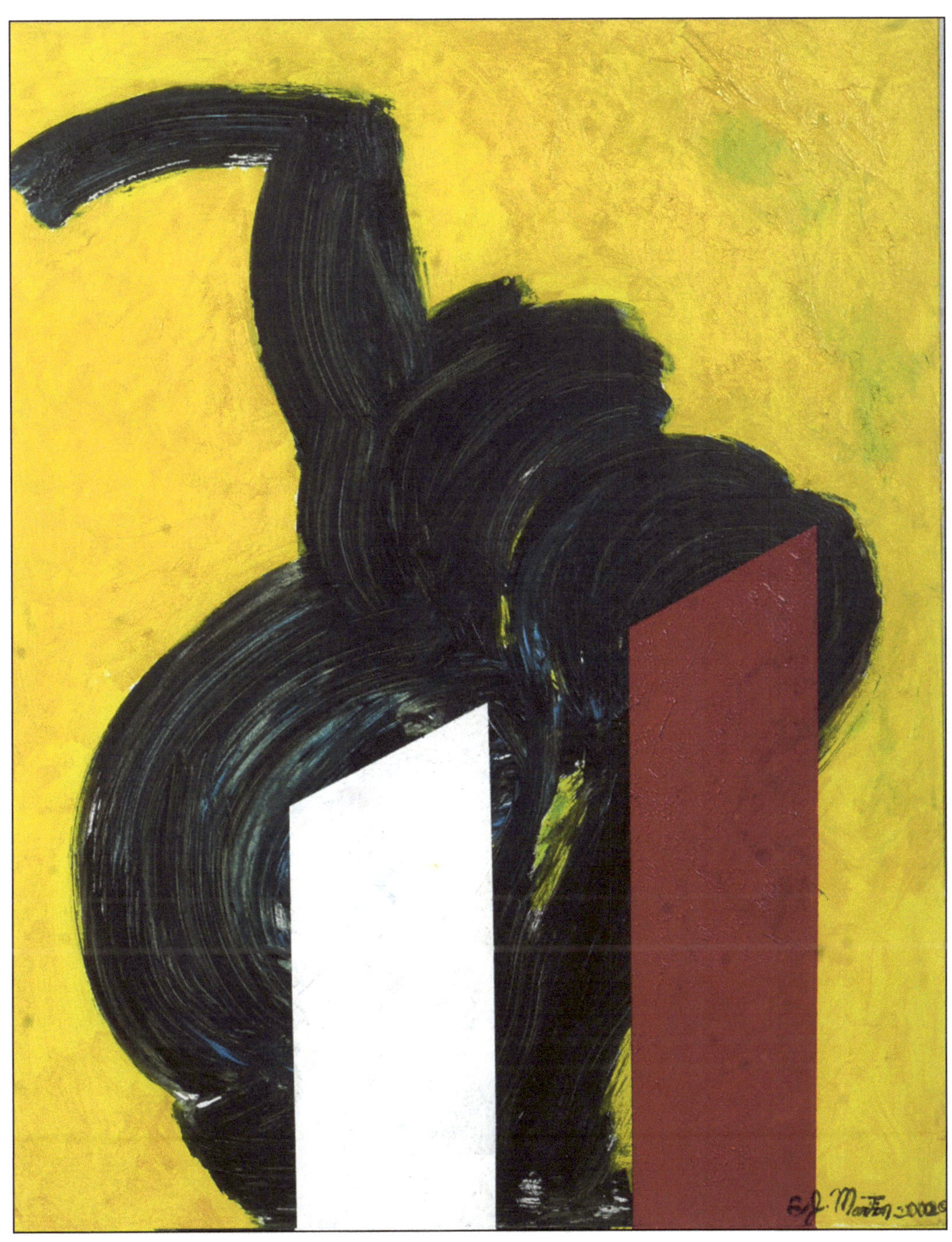

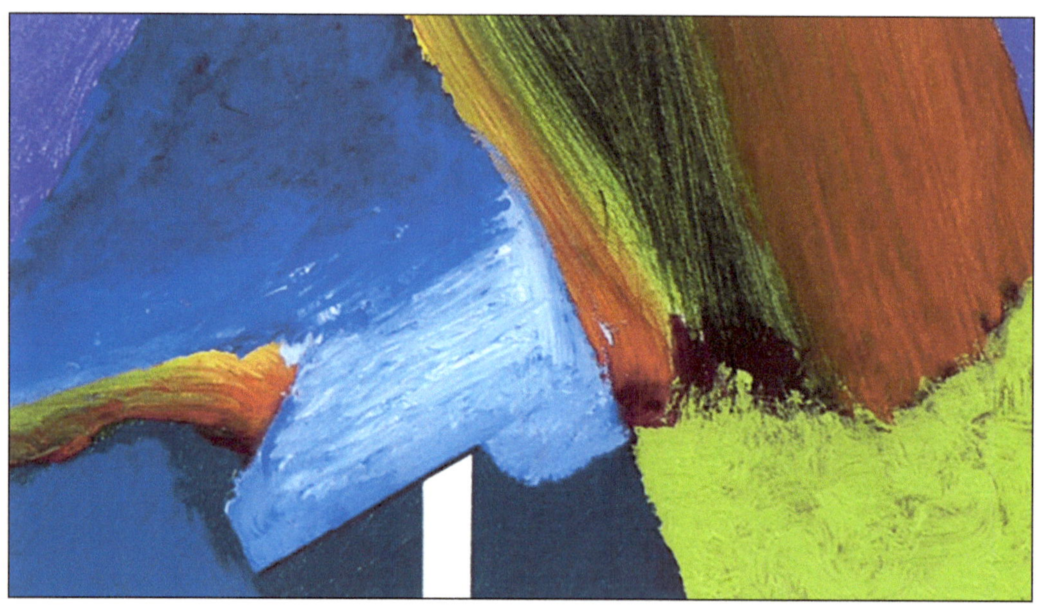

Untitled, 2000, acrylic on canvas (at right, close-up above), 30x24"

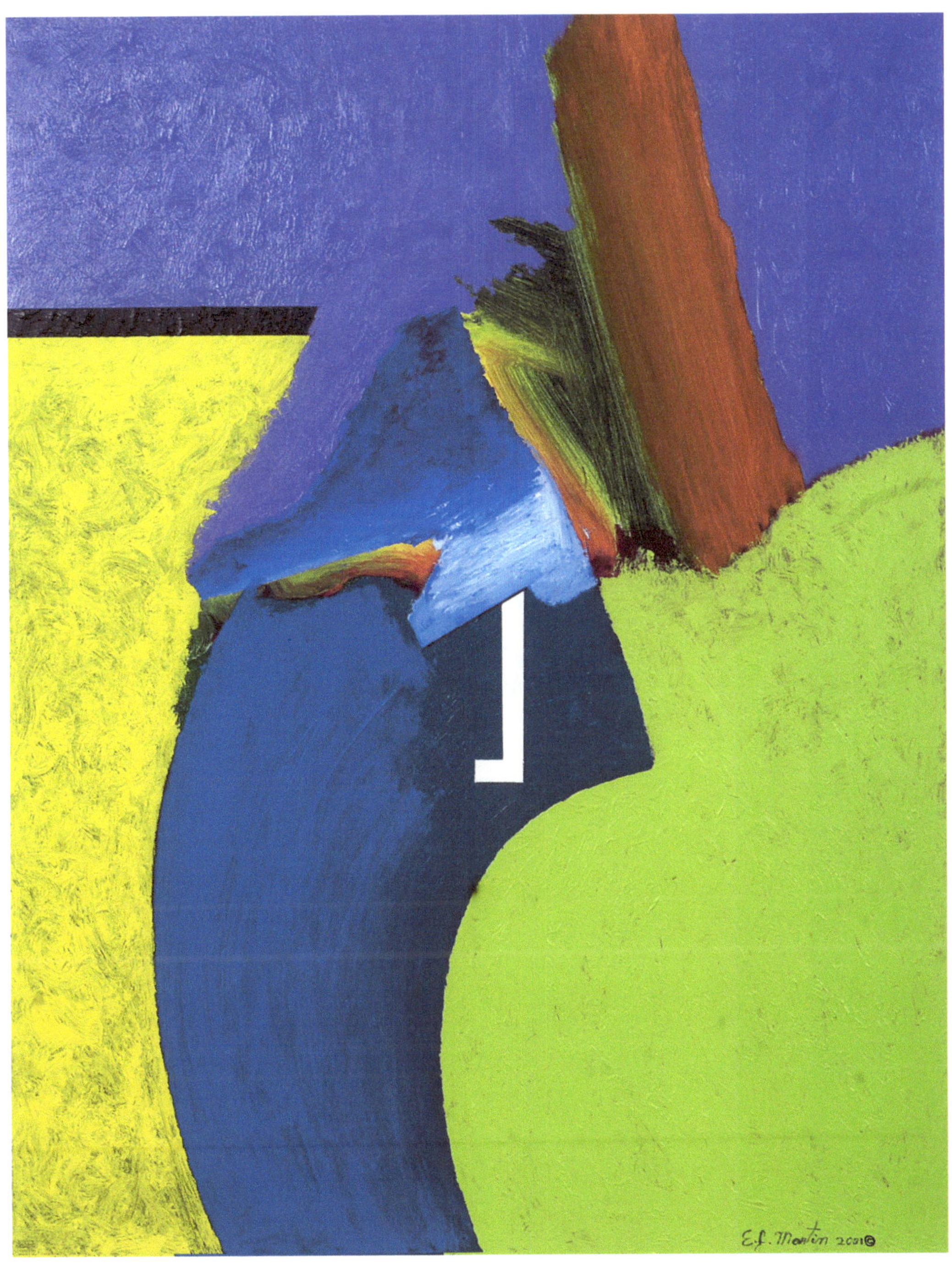
E.J. Martin 2001©

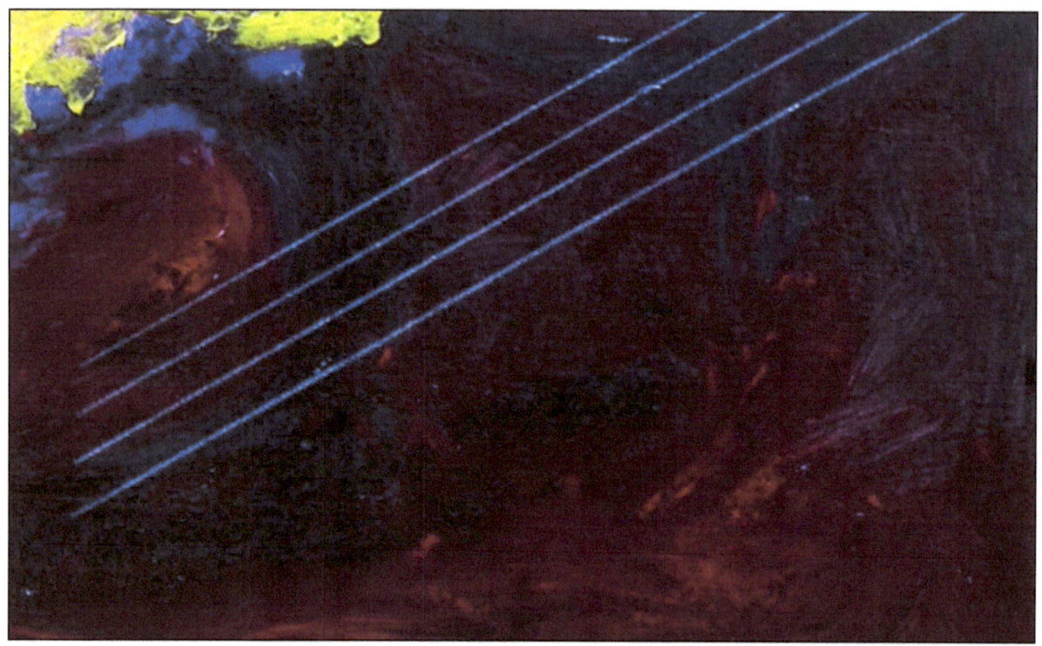

Untitled, 2000, acrylic on canvas (at right, close-up above), 30x24"

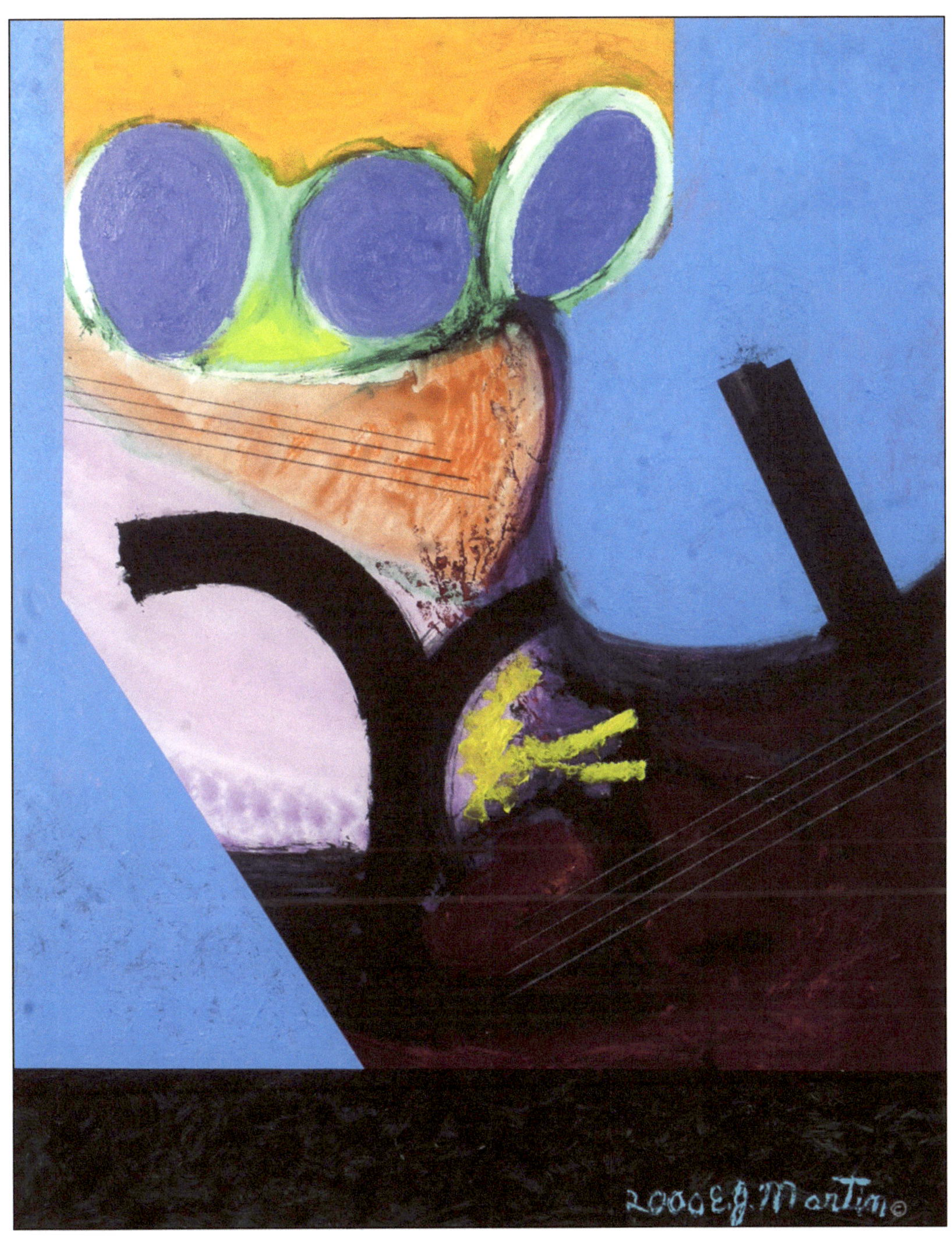
2000 E.J. Martin©

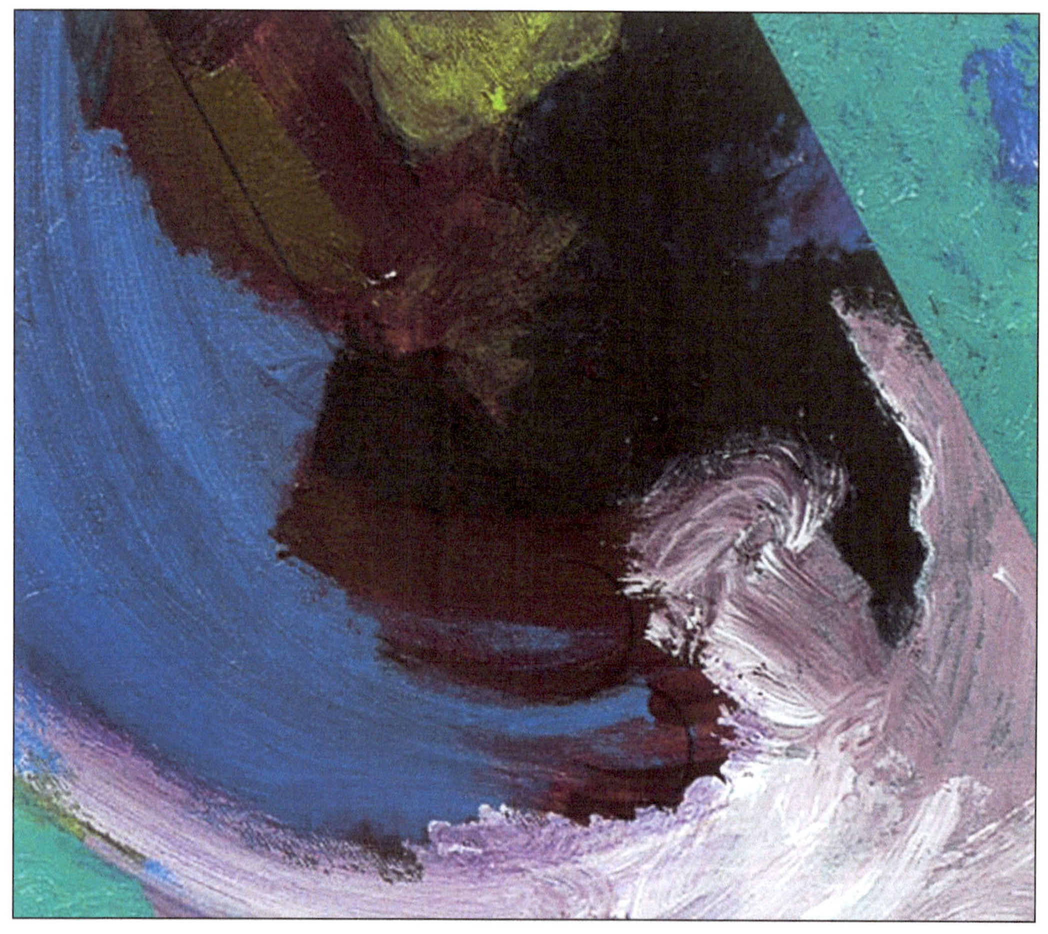

Untitled, 2000, acrylic on canvas (at right, close-up above), 30x24"

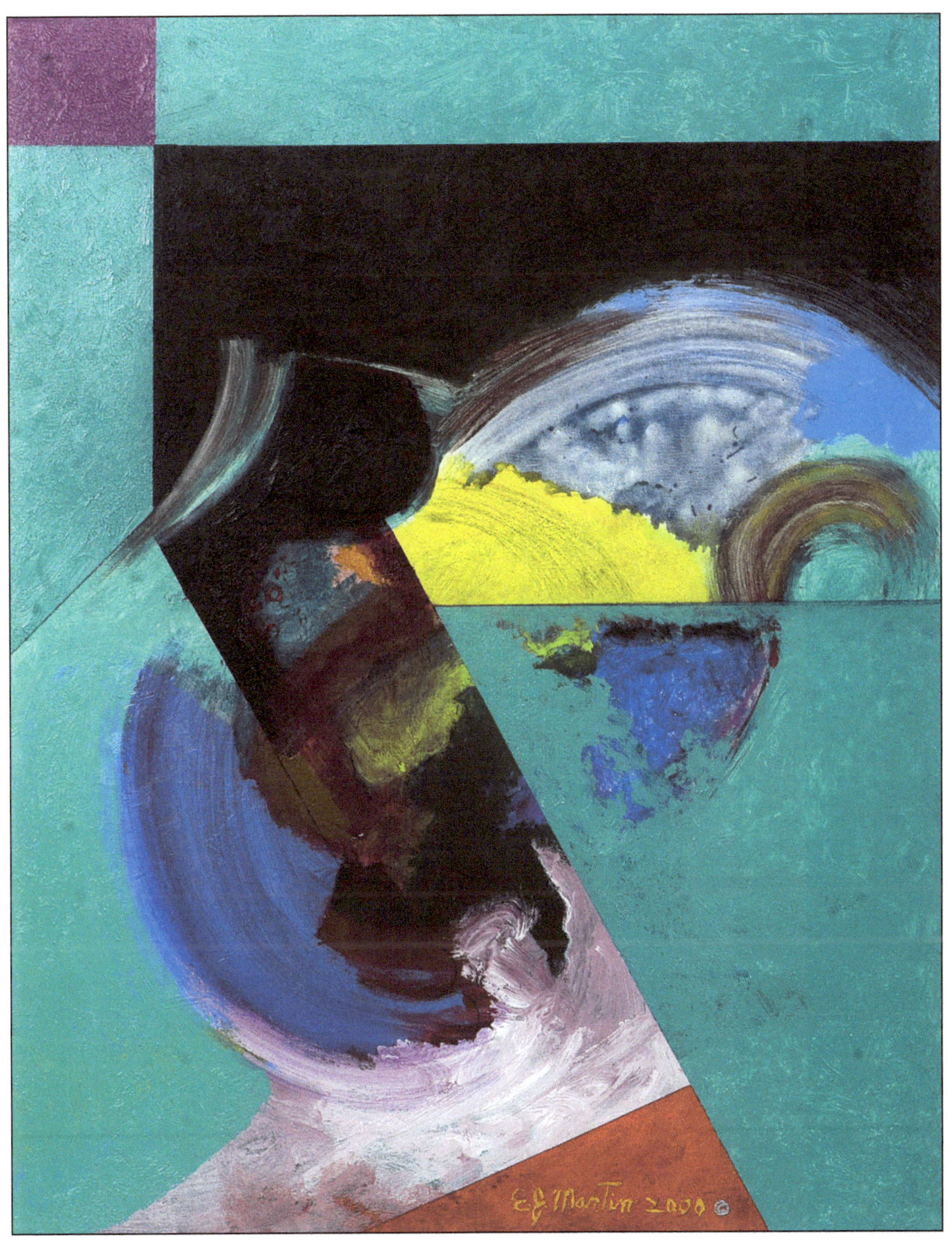

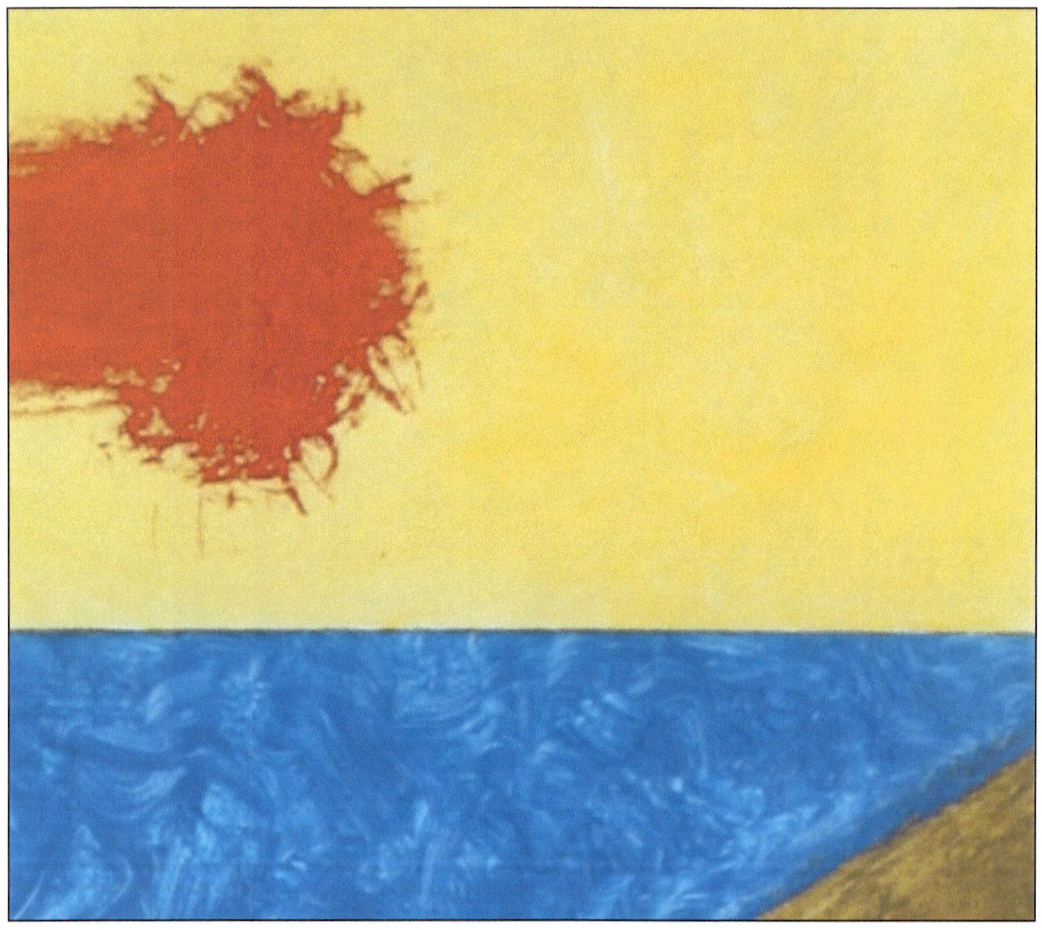

Untitled, 2000, acrylic on canvas (at right, close-up above), 30x24"

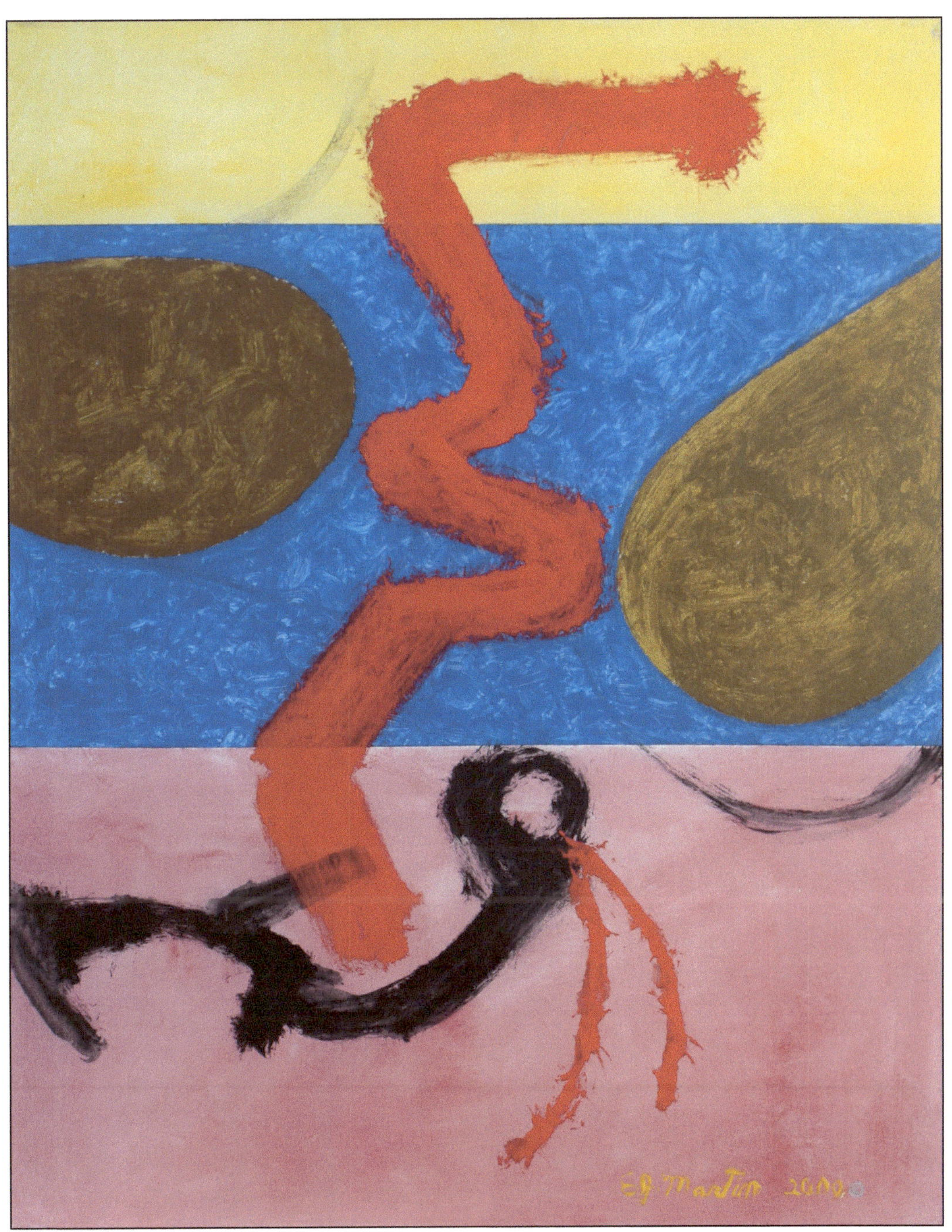

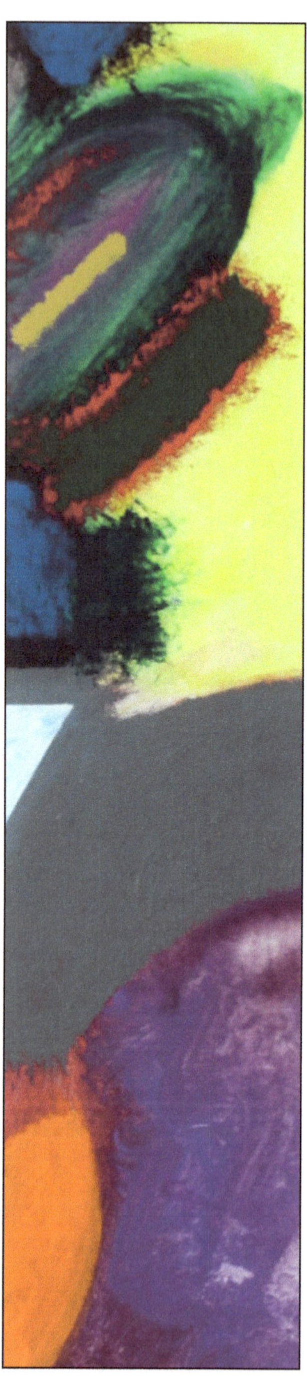

Untitled, 2000, acrylic on canvas (at right, close-up above), 30x24"

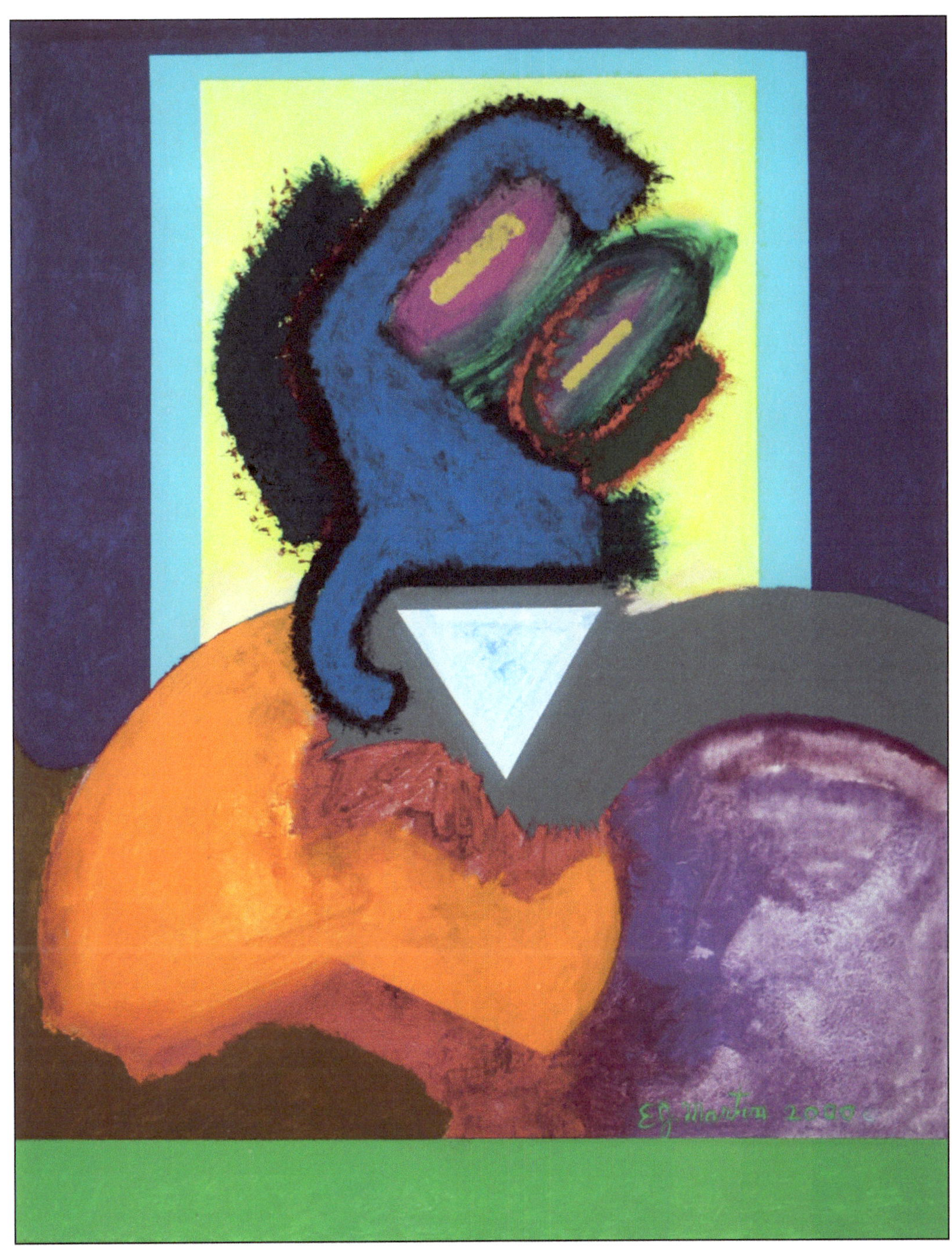

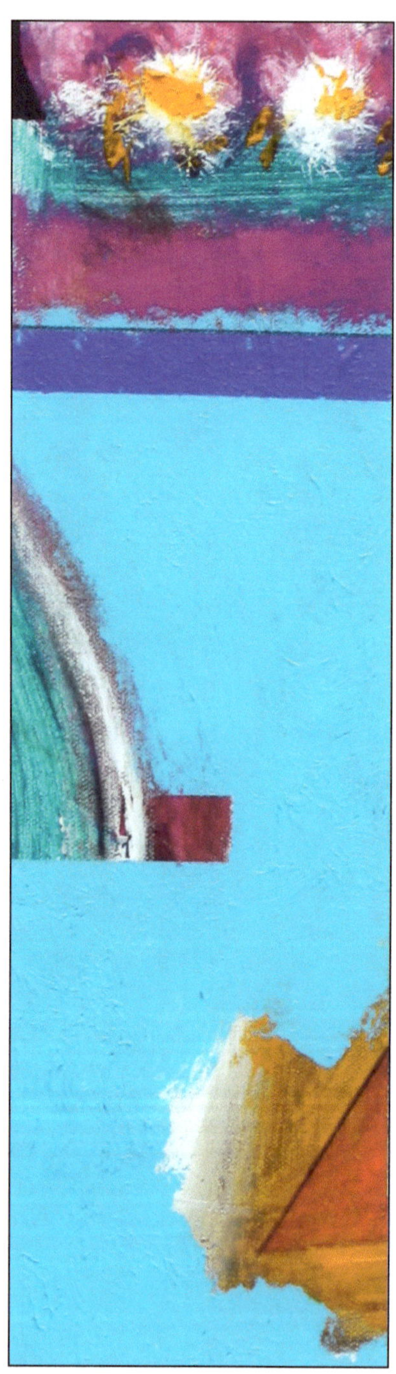

Untitled, 2000, acrylic on canvas (at right, close-up above), 30x24"

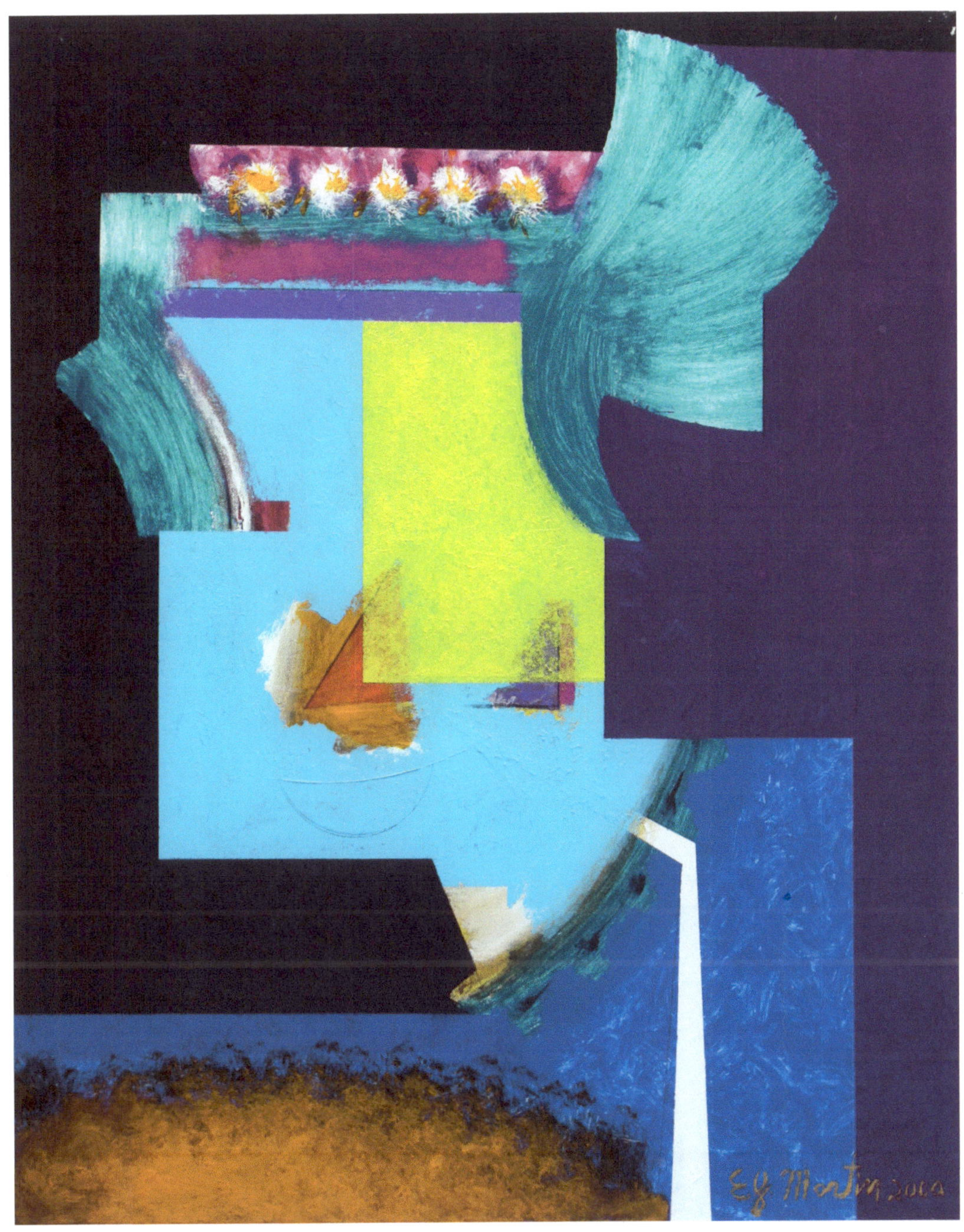
EJ Martin 2004

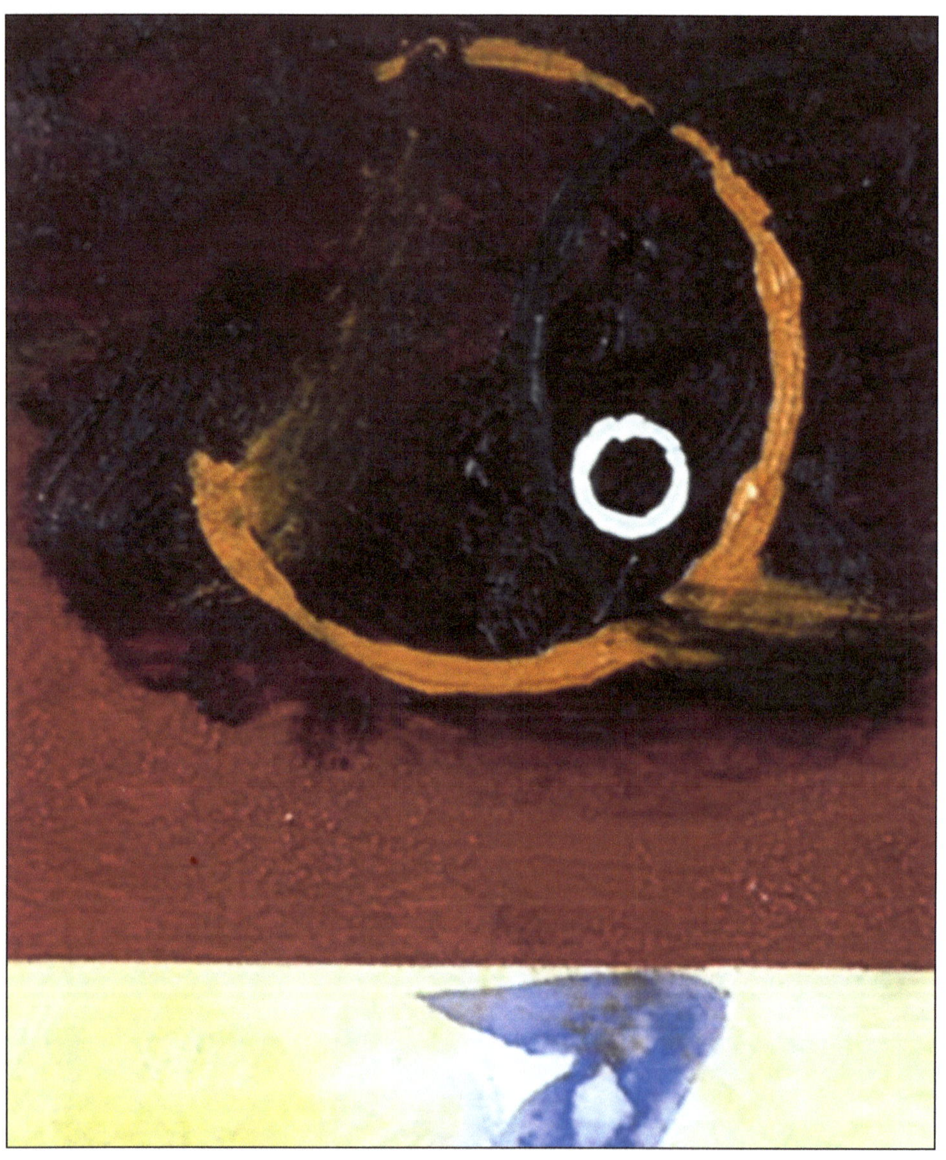

Untitled, 2000, acrylic on canvas (at right, close-up above), 30x24"

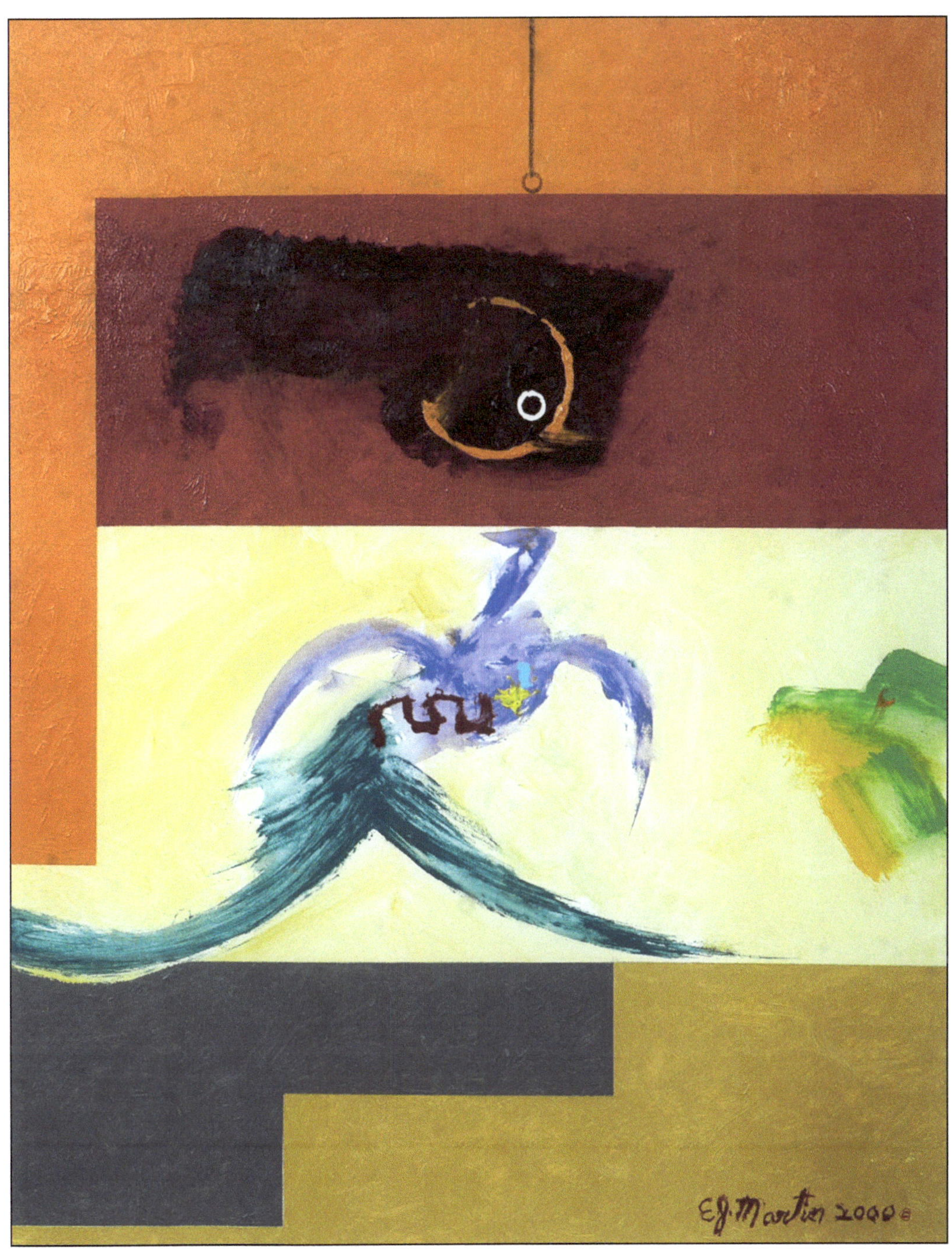
E.J. Martin 2000

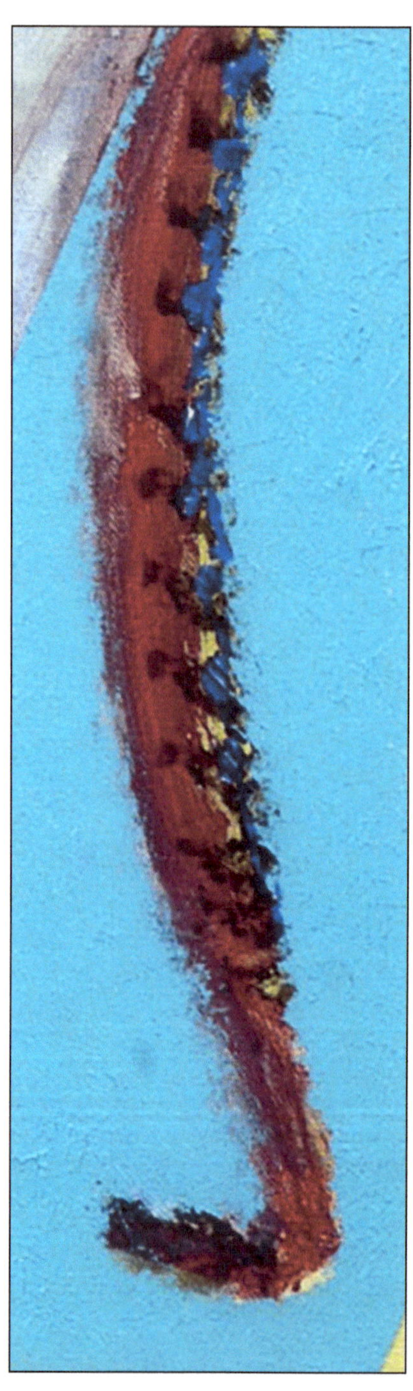

Untitled, 2000, acrylic on canvas (at right, close-up above), 30x24"

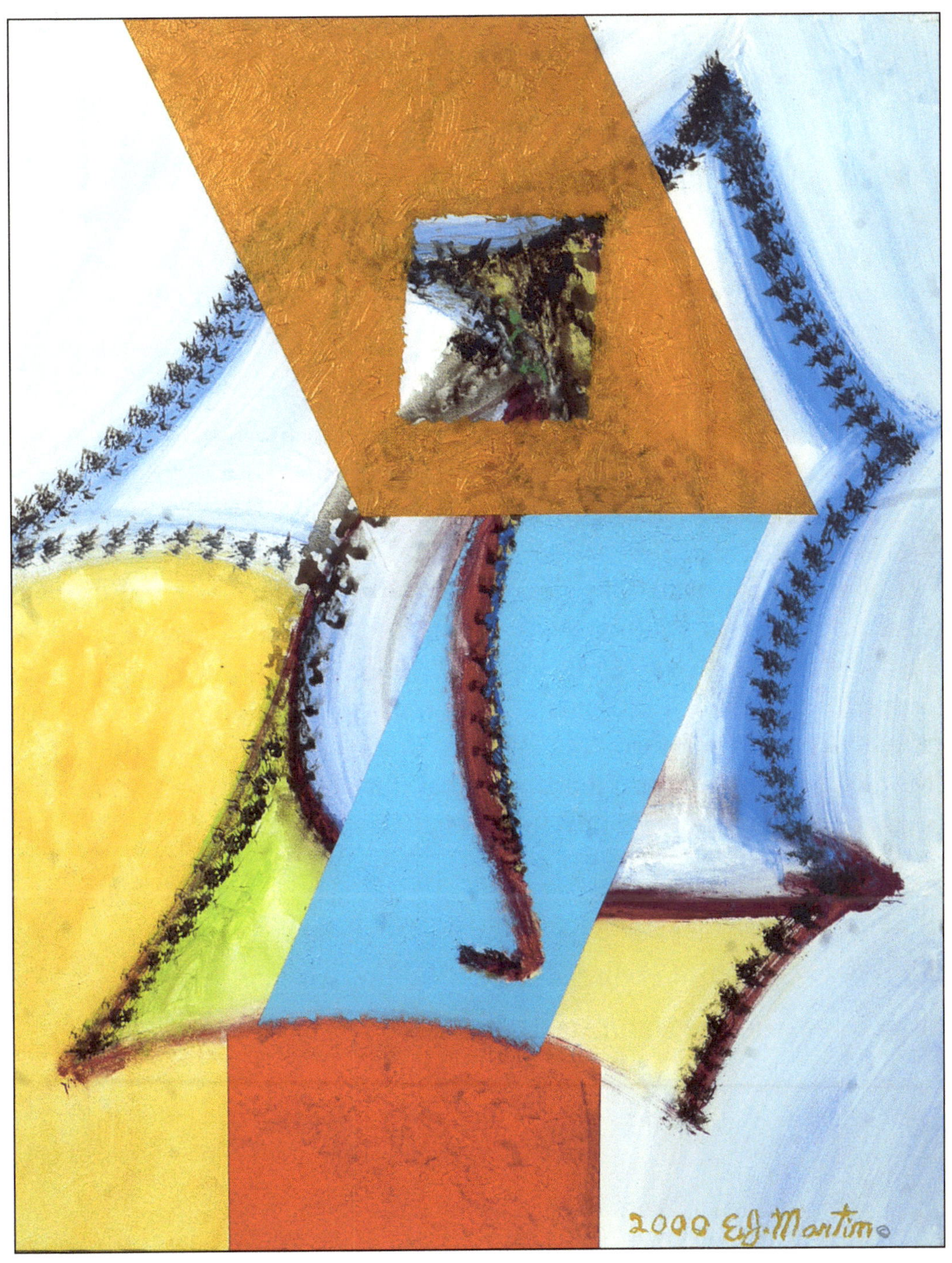
2000 E.J. Martin©

Eugene James Martin (b. Washington, D.C., July 24, 1938 - d. Lafayette, Louisiana, January 1, 2005) was a prolific African American visual artist.

Eugene J. Martin's art is best known for his imaginative, complex mixed media collages on paper, his often gently humorous pencil and pen and ink drawings, and his paintings on paper and canvas that may incorporate whimsical allusions to animal, machine and structural imagery among areas of "pure", constructed, biomorphic, or disciplined lyrical abstraction.

Eugene Martin's works of art can be found in numerous private art collections throughout the world, and are included in the permanent collection of the Ogden Museum of Southern Art, New Orleans; the Alexandria Museum of Art, Louisiana; the Stowitts Museum & Library in Pacific Grove, California; the Munich Museum of Modern Art; the Arthur Schomburg Center for Research in Black Culture, New York; the Mobile Museum of Art, Alabama; the Walter O. Evans Collection of African American Art in Savannah, Georgia, the Paul R. Jones Collection of African American Art at the University of Delaware, the Walter Anderson Museum of Art in Ocean Springs, Mississippi, and the Louisiana State University Museum of Art in the Shaw Center for the Arts in Baton Rouge, Louisiana.

http://www.artnet.com/awc/eugene-j-martin.html

http://www.artstor.org/what-is-artstor/w-html/col-martin.shtml

http://www.youtube.com/nemastoma

www.ingramcontent.com/pod-product-compliance
Lightning Source LLC
LaVergne TN
LVHW070142110826
845147LV00002B/309